ILLUSTRATIONS BY
SUSAN KUEHNL

FOREWORD BY
BRUCE DAVIDSON

HORSE SENSE

CAUSE AND CORRECTION OF HORSE AND RIDER PROBLEMS

KATE DELANO CONDAX

SIMON & SCHUSTER
New York   London   Toronto   Sydney   Tokyo   Singapore

For LDC and JB

With thanks to William Steinkraus,
George Morris, Vincent Dugan, and Steven D. Price

SIMON & SCHUSTER
Simon & Schuster Building
Rockefeller Center
1230 Avenue of the Americas
New York, New York 10020

Originally published by Winchester Press.

SIMON & SCHUSTER and colophon are registered trademarks of
Simon & Schuster Inc.

Designed by Mary Beth Kilkelly / Levavi & Levavi

Manufactured in the United States of America

3   5   7   9   10   8   6   4   2

Library of Congress Cataloging-in-Publication Data
Condax, Kate Delano.
Horse sense: cause and correction of horse and rider problems /
Kate Delano Condax; illustrations by Susan Kuehnl; foreword by
Bruce Davidson.
        p.   cm.
1. Horsemanship.   2. Horses—Behavior.
3. Horses—Training.   I. Title.
SF309.C65   1990
798.2—dc20   90-6965
            CIP
ISBN: 0-671-76335-0

CONTENTS

CONTENTS

FOREWORD

Who knows what makes someone a successful rider and competitor? People have made it to the top in the horse world from every possible angle.

Horse sense is not something one acquires easily. Time and experience teach most horse lovers how to cope with the routine problems of maintenance and serviceability. Time, however, is too often the one element not taken into account when dealing with horses. There is a good old horsemen's saying: "In order to go fast, one must go slow."

If riding is acknowledged as an art, it is clear that shortcuts are not the answer to obtaining the most complete, aesthetically pleasing, and productive result. Proper supervision is important right from the start; it helps beginners avoid some of the normal apprehensions and saves horses from the unnecessary discomfort caused by riders' ignorance. In this day and age, with good information available, there is no excuse for such ignorance.

I love my horses and would do anything to make them more comfortable and happier. As I think back on the years I've spent learning solutions to the basic problems everyone faces with horses, and how often I've needed guidance and advice in dealing with various problems, it often makes me wonder how I have persevered. I believe that in the world of horses, one has the best chance to develop a happy relationship through steady supervision and by reading constructive, informative literature, making *Horse Sense* invaluable to anyone who loves horses. Regardless of experience, there is always room to improve and expand.

—BRUCE DAVIDSON
World Champion Three-Day Event Rider

HORSE SENSE

INTRODUCTION

Have you ever ridden a horse who bucks, bolts, shies, pulls, stargazes, rears, or rushes his fences? Have you wondered why a horse persists in "bad" behavior despite your efforts to make him behave properly? This book can help you.

Here, listed in alphabetical order, is the clearest, most explicit instruction there is to solve the most common riding and handling problems. The book is arranged so that you can turn directly to the problems that most concern you and later read about the others at leisure.

This book is for the serious rider: the beginner who needs a safe and useful system for riding and working around horses; the intermediate who wants to refine his technique and become more effective; the expert who wants to compare his methods with those of other experts.

A "problem" is nothing more than behavior you don't want the horse to engage in. Often this behavior is perfectly natural from the horse's point of view. Or it may be that a previous owner has allowed the horse to learn habits you now want to change.

HORSE SENSE

In correcting a problem, it is most important that you know exactly what you intend to do before you begin correcting the horse. Otherwise you will confuse him and may make the problem even worse. But if you know exactly what to do, and carry out the correction calmly and systematically, most problems are not difficult to correct. This book will tell you how to get good results by following the instructions for each problem step by step. The instructions are explained in easy-to-understand, everyday language.

To ride well, and to work safely with horses, you need to understand why horses behave as they do. And you must know exactly what to do to change behavior that, although perfectly natural from a horse's point of view, is not acceptable while he is being ridden or when you are working around him.

This book will give you a general understanding of why horses do the things they do. Most important, it will give you specific instructions to correct problems.

There are many ways for a rider to solve any given problem. If one solution does not work, try another. Those given here are not the *only* ones, but they are all proven solutions that do work for intermediate to expert riders with most horses.

A horse who "misbehaves" is either:

1. Acting on instinct alone, as with unschooled, "green" horses
2. Afraid, confused, or in pain
3. Trying to get his own way, having learned that by resisting he can avoid doing what the rider wishes

If you can determine which of these causes underlies the horse's bad behavior, it will help you correct it. The cause is important, because you must never punish a frightened horse, or mistake confusion or pain for sheer refusal to obey. The section labeled "Cause" at the end of each section will help you decide the reason for the problem in each case. Keep in mind that for nearly every problem there is a solution; your job is to apply the best correction to each problem.

WHAT MAKES HORSES ACT THE WAY THEY DO?

Horses have strong instincts. You must understand these instincts in order to know how to work with horses, because although you can modify their reactions and behavior somewhat, you can never change their instincts. Beneath the training, they are always there.

From the days of the little dog-size ancestors of horses, natural enemies have preyed upon them. Horses act on the idea that it is "better to be safe than sorry" and will try to run away from anything that *might* be dangerous rather than take a chance by getting close to it.

Because horses who were too trusting were killed by predators, and those with a good healthy fear of danger were the only ones who survived to breed, for millions of years they passed this instinct from generation to generation. There is no instinct stronger in horses than to look for and run from danger.

That is why you may notice that your horse pricks his ears at small sounds in the woods, or appears to be looking into the distance when you ride. If he sees anything that frightens him (a piece of paper flapping in the wind, an umbrella, an unusual-looking building or machine) he may refuse to go forward. If the dangerous object (from his point of view) appears suddenly close at hand, he may take extreme measures to get away from it as quickly as possible—by bolting, rearing, or wheeling and kicking.

You may know that there is no danger in walking past a tractor in a field, or in crossing a garden hose. But the horse's instincts tell him that anything unusual is to be avoided. He will do what his instincts tell him unless you make his "natural" instinctive reaction difficult or unpleasant, and make a different reaction (what you want him to do) the easiest and most pleasant thing for him to do. *This is the basis for all schooling.*

Besides the instinct to run from danger, another strong instinct is "herd instinct." There is safety in numbers, since any one of the group may alert the others to danger. In a field of resting horses, one will usually remain standing, keeping watch while the others lie down. Horses grazing in a field will stick together, or go off in little bunches. This same herd instinct makes your horse balk at being asked to leave the stable or to leave other horses when you are riding, or it may make him hurry to get back to the barn after a ride.

In a herd, a "pecking order" is quickly established. From earliest times, the strongest and smartest horse controlled the herd, since herds with weak or stupid leaders didn't survive. The top horse can bite or kick anyone else; the horse below him can bite or kick anyone except the top horse, and so on, down to the bottom horse, who doesn't get to pick on anyone at all and has to stay out of the way of everybody. Once the order has been established, there is usually little fighting among the herd members unless a strange horse is introduced into the same field. Then the newcomer must find his own place in the pecking order by biting, kicking, or running away from the other horses.

Horses being ridden have exactly the same instincts, and may want to bite or kick another horse who comes alongside them if they feel the newcomer is their social inferior. Of course, you must modify this instinctive behavior since it is not acceptable for a horse being ridden to bite or kick.

Sometimes horses do things that people may consider stupid—but which are actually perfectly logical when seen from the horse's point of view. What makes a horse run back into his stall when the barn is on fire and he has just been led outside to safety? To a horse, his stall is a place of quiet, comfort, and safety; here he has his feed and hay, here he spends his peaceful nights. In the case of a barn fire a horse seeks to escape the terror of noise, smoke, confusion, and rough handling by running back to the one place where, experience has always taught him, he will find safety.

Horses are very curious. If they are safe and do not feel threatened they will try to find out how things work, what things are made of, and what other animals—including people—will do in various circumstances. Horses look things over from a safe distance first, and then if all seems well, come closer for a better look and smell, and finally a nuzzle and perhaps a taste. Horses use their lips almost as hands—to see how something can be moved about (they learn to open latches on stable gates and doors this way) or to see what something is made of. Once a horse has made a preliminary investigation with his lips, he will usually try to bite anything he finds interesting or attractive; this may include your clothing or your body or a piece of tack left sitting on the rail of his pasture. This has nothing to do with meanness or an attempt to be "naughty"—he is simply finding out about his world. In the same way, a young horse will play with others, biting, kicking, rearing, and racing around. None of this is meant to harm his fellows; he is only learning to use his body and sharpen his timing and reflexes.

This same curiosity makes it possible to school a horse to do things that are not, to him, natural. A horse will try to find the easiest, most pleasant solution to any problem. So, if he finds that stubborn refusal to go forward earns him vigorous use of leg by the rider and a swift smack with a whip, he will decide it is more dangerous to refuse to go forward than to pass a dangerous-looking tractor in a field.

In more advanced levels of schooling, curiosity will cause a horse to try many different responses to a signal from the rider until he finds the one that "works"—that is, causes the rider to stop giving the signal.

For instance, a horse learning to canter on either lead on signal may try several answers to the rider's signal: He may try to run away from the signal by going faster; he may canter on the "wrong" lead (because both leads, as far as the horse is concerned, are equally correct); he may canter with one lead in front and another behind (disunited); he may buck; he may break to a trot; he may put his head as high as it will go; he may balk and refuse to go freely forward. As a rule, the more intelligent a horse is, the greater number of different responses he will try as answers to any signal he does not understand. You teach him what the correct response is by rewarding him when he does what you want, and by repeating the signal each time he does something other than what you want. *A reward consists of ceasing to give the signal. The better the rider, the more alert he will be to the moment the horse responds correctly, and the sooner he will reward the horse.*

The aim in working with horses is first to make them safe and pleasant to work around and to ride, and then to bring out the best movement of which a particular horse is capable. Horses, like people, differ greatly in the way they look and move. You cannot take a short-legged, heavily built pony and expect him to move as fluidly as a thoroughbred, for instance. But you *can* develop his potential to its fullest, and make him the best-educated, best-moving animal that nature allows.

Some horses, by physical construction and personality, are better suited than others to particular kinds of work. A horse who regularly jumps out of his pasture just for the fun of it to go visiting his friends next door will make a better jumper than the horse who dangles his front legs over even a small fence—thus having to hoist his body higher into the air than a horse who tucks up his legs well—and finds jumping tiring and difficult as a result. A very lazy and sluggish pony will make a better mount for a young child without any experience in riding than a lively, energy-filled pony. A good horseman chooses a horse carefully and does not try to fit a round peg into a square hole. But a novice, buying a horse for the first time, may choose a horse for his color or pretty head without regard for the much more important question of what purpose the horse will be put to. If you have any doubts, it is best to consult an experienced person.

Horses have excellent memories. Once they have learned something they will never forget it. For this reason it is very important to *teach your horse carefully, a step at a time.* If you try to teach too much new work to a horse in a single session, he will become confused and tired and will associate work and new lessons with unpleasantness. When starting difficult, new lessons, work for short periods of time, perhaps ten minutes, then give your horse a rest by walking him on a long loose rein for five minutes before beginning a new session.

When a horse is working well it is tempting to keep on working, but don't. Stop while you are ahead. If you keep on practicing until he becomes tired and begins making mistakes, he will remember those mistakes after you have put him back in the stable. It is better to stop while he is still doing well in his new work and let him think about *that* until the next time you ride him. A good plan is to *school* your horse (teach new work or repeat partly learned exercises) in moderation, and then *exercise* him (ride outside cross-country giving as few commands as possible) so the horse does not become overtired mentally, yet remains physically fit.

A good horseman *never* loses his temper. He knows what to do to correct any problem, then systematically and calmly proceeds to carry out his corrections (although with considerable force when necessary).

A rider who is not entirely clear himself about what to do cannot possibly explain to a horse what he expects of him. If you are not sure what to do about a problem, *find out first*, then begin correcting it. Trial and error attempts by a rider are very harmful, because the horse remembers everything you do, and you cannot later say to a horse, "Oh, I didn't mean that signal I just gave you. Forget about all that and pay attention to this signal instead."

The horse's hindquarters contain by far the most powerful set of muscles he has. Horses can move their hind legs not only backward and forward, like the forelegs, but sideways too; the greatest power and mobility come from the hind legs. Keeping this principle in mind will help you understand how to bring out the best movement in your horse. You must use this power and mobility in schooling; if a horse does a transition from a canter to a walk and does not use his hind legs very much to do so, the transition is jolting and awkward. If he uses his hind legs a great deal, the resulting transition is smooth and coordinated. A horse playing freely in a field automatically knows how to engage his hind legs for a smooth stop, but with a rider on his back, asking him to do things he does not fully understand, he may fail to use his hind legs properly. The educated rider then knows to tell the horse to use his hind legs by squeezing with his own legs. An interesting experiment can show you how much difference it makes in terms of smoothness when a horse engages his hind legs and when he does not: Trot down a steep hill, sitting to the trot. The horse plows along with his weight on the front legs, and you will find the trot very jolting. Next, trot *up* the same hill. The horse must now use his hind legs a great deal, engaging his hocks to push and carry himself up the hill. You will find the trot very smooth and easy to sit to.

The objectives to strive for in all your work are:

1. *Forward.* The horse must move freely forward whenever asked, without resistance. This is of utmost importance.
2. *Straight.* The horse's backbone must be straight from head to tail when moving on a straight line, and curved when he moves on a curved line, to the same degree as the turn or circle.

3. *Rhythm.* The rhythm of the horse's steps must remain the same until you ask for a faster or slower rhythm or a new gait.
4. *Calm.* The horse must remain calmly alert without confusion or fear.

When treated kindly and fairly, horses are affectionate and generous animals. Never give the horse an impossible or unreasonable command, always insist that he do what you ask, and immediately reward him by ceasing to give the command. His calmness will come from his knowing that he can do what you want, that he must do it, and will be rewarded immediately by cessation of the signal when he obeys. If you know what you want, give a clear signal, always use the same signal to mean the same thing, and reward promptly, your horse will gain confidence in your judgment.

This confidence makes it possible for him to obey you even if his instincts tell him to do something else.

A GOOD INSTRUCTOR— WHAT TO LOOK FOR, HOW TO FIND ONE

The first thing you must learn is proper *form*. This simply means learning to position your body so that your weight, hands, legs, and balance are in the most convenient and effective places for you to give signals to the horse and to move with him when he moves. For different work you will sit and move differently: When you jump or gallop you sit differently from when you walk your horse on a loose rein, for instance.

Second, you must learn the aids—that is, the *mechanics* of giving signals—for instance, pulling the rein in this direction and squeezing with that leg to get a certain result. The aids are fairly scientific, consisting of signals that have proved themselves effective when applied to the horse's physical action and general mentality.

The third and by far most interesting part of your education as a rider involves learning to judge *timing* and *amount*—that is, at what precise moment should you give a certain signal, how gently or forcefully, and for how long. It is here that the *art* in riding begins.

HORSE SENSE

A rider who learns only form and mechanics of giving the aids but who lacks sensitivity in judging timing and amount will be a mere passenger on the horse. His position will look fine, but he will not be capable of bringing out the best work the horse can do. A horse ridden by such a person will not perform as well as for a really good rider. When a good rider gets on, the horse automatically seems to move perfectly, where a moment earlier he was moving badly with the passenger-rider. This is not mysterious: The good rider simply gives a multitude of small corrections to the horse the instant they become necessary. The good rider feels this moment before it can be seen by someone watching, and corrects the problem early so it never even becomes apparent to an observer. But the passenger-rider, who lacks skill and whose perception is less sharp, does not feel the problem arise until the horse is already carrying out the undesired behavior. By the time the passenger-rider realizes there is a problem, it is too late to correct it smoothly or at all.

You should find an instructor who can give you good guidance in all three areas of learning—form, mechanics of the aids, and development of a good sense of timing and amount.

An instructor will show you step by step how to build a "language" between you and your horse. This language is learned through a series of exercises that you will practice with your instructor until you are skilled enough to practice alone. Your instructor will also answer specific questions about your horse's behavior or misbehavior.

Try to find an instructor who has trained in *dressage* (the word simply means "training" in French) because dressage is a *coordinated system of signals*. Many self-taught riders have, by hit-or-miss, found tricks that work well enough for some things but cannot work beyond a certain point because they will conflict with the next set of signals that must be used. For example, if you teach a horse to canter by turning his head to the outside rail, he will stumble onto the proper lead surely enough. But if you later want to teach him to canter on a very small circle, he will find it difficult to strike off on a small circle to the left while the rider pulls his head to the right to make him take the correct lead. Dressage, however, because it is a carefully thought-out coordinated system of signals, avoids such contradictions. In addition, dressage has the advantage of being—with some minor variations—an international language between horse and rider. You could get on a horse in any country in the world, and if he were properly schooled in dressage, "talk" to him using the same signals you use at home.

A reliable place to find recommendations for a teacher is the Pony Club. This includes not only ponies as the name might suggest, but horses too. Pony Clubs exist throughout the United States and England, so you can probably find one near you. Write to:

United States Pony Clubs, Inc.
303 South High Street
West Chester, Pennsylvania 19380

Another source of information is the United States Combined Training Association. The USCTA sponsors combined training events, a type of competition in which the same horse competes in three separate tests, the best overall score winning. The first day (or phase—sometimes the entire three tests are held on one day) is a dressage test. This is a precise set of movements at walk, trot, canter, and sometimes high-school movements, depending on the level of the test. The second day is cross-country, which involves galloping over hills and fields and through woods, jumping solid "rustic" fences and water. The last day is stadium jumping, which involves jumping fences like those found in horse-show jumping or hunter classes.

The emphasis in combined training is on development of the horse to his fullest potential. It does not matter if you have the most beautiful, or the most expensive, horse; it is a contest of effective riding and good schooling. For detailed information write to:

HORSE SENSE

The United States Combined Training Association
1 Winthrop Square
Boston, Massachusetts 02110

For riders interested in western schooling and equitation, each of the following organizations will provide information:

The National Education Association
National Riding Committee—Western Division
1400 Rolling Hills Drive
Graham, Texas 76046

The National Horse and Pony Youth Activities Council
5052 Thatcher Road
Ojai, California 93023

The National Cutting Horse Association
P.O. Box 12155
Fort Worth, Texas 76116

EQUIPMENT

BRIDLE

All the corrections given in this book were carried out using a simple hollow-mouth egg-butt snaffle, the mildest bit there is. The horses ranged from very green young horses to badly spoiled older horses with firmly entrenched bad habits.

The best policy is to use a mild bit and school your horse so he is easy to ride in it. If necessary, stay in an enclosed area—a ring or a small field—until you are sure that you can stop and turn your horse easily, then take him outside and repeat the same work.

When choosing a bit, make sure the corners of the mouth are not squeezed in by a bit that is too narrow. The leather parts of the bridle should be the right size so they do not pinch or bind. Adjust the bit so it barely wrinkles the corners of the horse's mouth.

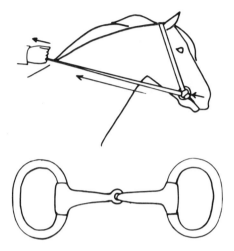

Top: Direct action of snaffle bit.

Bottom: Hollow-mouth egg-butt snaffle bit.

SADDLE

A forward-seat saddle is designed for both riding on the flat and jumping. One without knee rolls is preferable to one with thick padding between your legs and the horse, as it will put you closer to the horse. Look at the saddle from the side; when it is on your horse the deepest part of the seat must not be farther than halfway back—otherwise the saddle will make you sit too far back. This is important, because if you sit too far back your legs will be too far in front of you and you will be off balance and therefore find it difficult to give proper leg signals. Imagine two examples: First, you are standing on the ground, your knees slightly bent, your feet 2½ feet apart; second, you are sitting in a chair with your feet on the floor in front of you. The first example is the position you should be in when you are sitting in a saddle; if your saddle puts your weight too far back you will be like the second example.

Use an elastic-end leather girth, which does not pinch the

horse, expands when he breathes, and is easy for the rider to do up.

MARTINGALE

A martingale is a preventive measure, not really a cure for the problem of the horse raising his head too high, because when you remove the martingale the problem is usually still there. However, sometimes a martingale is useful, as for example on young horses ridden outside a ring for the first few times, or on a strong horse with a known tendency to bolt. But in the end, the only real solution to the problems helped temporarily by a martingale is proper schooling or reschooling. If a martingale is used, a plain standing martingale is good, as it attaches to the nose-band of the bridle and simply prevents the horse from raising his head, without interfering with the rider's use of the reins to give signals.

WHIP

Always carry a whip when you ride. The best-mannered horse will, sometimes, decide not to go forward, and one swift swat with a whip can prevent momentary hesitation from becoming a vice. The whip should be stiff although flexible, (not "rubbery" or overly bendable). A dressage whip or gaited horse whip, about three feet long, is useful for schooling (although you cannot properly carry one in a show ring) since in many cases you can use it without taking your hand off the rein. If you use a jumping bat—a short, stiff whip with a broad leather "popper" at the end that makes a smacking noise when it strikes the horse—be sure it is long enough to reach comfortably from your hand across your knee while riding, with six inches or more extending beyond the knee.

HORSE SENSE

SPURS

Until you are absolutely certain that you will *never* accidentally dig your spurs into the horse's side if he should buck, shy, prop, or swerve, it is a good idea *not* to wear spurs. A whip will do the same job—reinforce your leg signal if it is not obeyed willingly—and an accidental jab with a spur can cause serious difficulties. If you do wear spurs, when you are sure you are ready, use either dulled round ones or flat blunt ones, ½ inch or shorter.

TERMS USED IN THIS BOOK

GOOD HANDS

You often hear the term "good hands," but what exactly does this mean? What do good hands do? How can you develop them?

Good hands do the following:

- Give the correct signal clearly to the horse, at the right moment
- Use as light a signal as possible, but as strong as necessary to get the correct response
- Most important, *when the horse obeys, stop giving the signal*

These points raise a number of questions. What is the "correct signal"? What is the "right moment"? How can you be sure if the horse is giving the "correct response"?

These questions are best answered by looking at specific

exercises you will use to school your horse. For each exercise there are signals that tell the horse to respond in a particular way. There are specific things you must do to enforce the signal if it is not obeyed.

There is a particular instant when you must give the signal, based on the horse's balance, where he is placing his feet, the curve of his backbone, and a number of other factors that are different in each case.

SOFTEN THE HAND

To soften the hand, move your whole hand holding the rein slightly forward, or merely open your fingers for an instant before closing them again, thereby removing pressure on the bit momentarily. The purpose of softening the hand is to acknowledge some correct movement by the horse, and to reward him for it.

SNATCH

The snatch is a punishment used to reinforce a signal that has not been obeyed, or to correct a very firmly established bad habit. To snatch the rein, first release it forward slightly so there is some slack, then jerk it abruptly. The rein (or a lead shank) can be snatched upward, backward, or downward. In each case, the effect will be to startle the horse, so that he ceases momentarily to do what he is doing.

The snatch generally causes the horse's head to move in the opposite direction from the snatch. If you snatch downward with a lead shank, a horse will raise his head.

The key is abruptness. You must make the action so quick that the horse cannot pull against it.

TERMS USED IN THIS BOOK

INSIDE, OUTSIDE

Inside refers to the inside of a turn or circle, outside to the outside of a turn or circle. On a circle going to the right, the inside rein is the right rein, the inside leg the right leg.

SEQUENCE OF FOOTFALLS AT THE WALK, TROT, CANTER, AND REINBACK

The sequence (or order) in which the horse puts down his feet is important to understand and to recognize when you are riding, because there is a specific moment when you must give every signal to a horse for the best result, and you must be able to recognize that moment.

- *Walk* (four beats). Left hind, left fore, right hind, right fore (the sequence may begin with any foot).
- *Trot* (two beats). The legs move in pairs: the right hind and left fore (left diagonal pair) followed by the left hind and right fore (right diagonal pair) or vice versa.
- *Canter* (three beats). For canter on left lead: Right hind, then both the left hind and right fore at the same time, then the left (leading) foreleg, followed by a moment of suspension during which all four feet are in the air.
- *Reinback* (two beats). The legs move in diagonal pairs, exactly like the trot only the horse moves backward instead of forward. Left hind and right fore at the same time, then right hind and left fore, or vice versa.

HORSE SENSE

The **direct rein** moves in a sideways and slightly forward direction "leading" the horse in the way you want to go. The right direct rein is put into effect by the rider moving his right hand to the right and a little forward—that is, away from the horse's shoulder and toward the right. Put slight pressure on the rein, but in a sideways direction, not backward. The horse bends toward the rein; there is no slowing of the forward movement.

The **indirect rein** either resists or moves in a slightly backward direction, moving on a line from the horse's mouth diagonally so that it would, if the rein were long enough, cross the horse's withers. However, the rider holds the rein in front of the withers and simply moves his hand in a diagonal direction; his hand will not actually cross the withers (if it does, the reins are too long). The right indirect rein will cause the horse to bend his head and neck to the right, and, depending on what other signals are given, cause him to move his body in various ways (see each specific exercise for exactly how). The indirect rein tends to slow the horse's forward movement somewhat.

The **opposing rein** (direct rein of opposition) moves parallel to the horse, straight back. It tends to slow the forward movement as well as to prevent the head from turning away from it. Depending upon what other signals are given, it causes the horse to move his body in various ways.

There are other rein effects, but these are all you will need for the corrections in this book.

ALPHABETICAL
LISTING
OF PROBLEMS

ABOVE THE BIT—"STARGAZING"

A horse is above the bit when he *raises* his head in response to pressure on the reins by the rider. Sometimes the horse may raise his head very high, sometimes only slightly. But in either case, if he raises his head when he feels rein pressure (instead of lowering it slightly and bringing in his chin slightly) he is above the bit, and this is a fault.

To make the horse lower his head, raise your hands *higher* than his mouth—about five or six inches above the normal position (that is, above the straight line from elbow to bit). Put a steady pressure on both reins while in this position.

When the horse responds with any downward movement, however slight—he may just nod or bob his head slightly the first few times—reward him by softening your hand immediately (move your hands forward slightly or merely open the fingers briefly in order to remove the pressure from the reins momentarily). You must reward him for any attempt to lower his head, even if he raises it again right away. The key is to repeat the exercise until he learns that there will be a constant unpleasant pressure on the reins until he lowers his head, and that the only way he can prevent the pressure on his mouth is to keep his head in a normal position and not raise his head above the bit.

Remember to maintain the same speed and rhythm you were working in, as pressure on the reins tends to make the horse slow down unless accompanied by enough leg pressure (or whip if needed) to counteract it. If, for instance, you are trotting at a medium speed, do not let the horse go into a slow trot or walk when he feels you apply rein pressure. The *only* change you must allow him to make is to lower his head.

You cannot pull a horse's head down. The more you pull downward, the higher he will raise his head to try to escape the bit, since a horse naturally pulls in the opposite direction from anything he finds unpleasant.

Cause:

- The rider pulling a horse's head downward if the horse has any tendency to raise it
- An attempt by the horse to avoid doing something he finds confusing or dislikes
- Conformation faults—long back, short neck, for example— may predispose a horse to raise his head and neck in an effort to balance himself

BALKING—"NAPPY"

At the first sign of unwillingness to go forward, use your legs and at the same time apply the whip forcefully once or twice right behind your calf. Always carry a whip when you ride, because

ABOVE THE BIT.

Top: Incorrect—rider's hands too low.

Lower left: Correct—rider's hands higher than horse's mouth.

Lower right: Correct—rider's hands yield as horse lowers and extends head.

even the best-behaved horse may refuse to go forward sometimes, and if this behavior goes uncorrected, it will quickly become a vice. If you hold your whip not in the usual way (that is, hanging down) but rather turn it in your hand so that the major part of it is pointing into the air, you can hit much harder (see illustration, page 64). While using the whip, maintain contact with the horse's mouth with both reins in one hand, and use the free hand to hit. Then take one rein in each hand as usual.

Once the horse moves forward, speak encouragingly to him. Keep him in a strong trot or a canter for at least several yards before coming back to a walk. Be on the alert for renewed signs of balking because he will almost certainly attempt to stop again. Keep your hands about 10 inches apart and well in front of you (usually one-third to one-half the way up the horse's neck) to prevent his wheeling, and maintain light contact with his mouth at all times. Instant, energetic correction, repeated as often as necessary, will cure this problem.

If the horse shows any tendency to rear, increase the signals that drive him forward. You may want to use a standing martingale adjusted tightly enough so he cannot raise his head enough to rear (see illustration of martingale, page 35, and Rearing, page 95).

Cause:

- ♦ Fear of something that appears dangerous to him
- ♦ If the rider allows the horse to refuse to go forward even once, the behavior is quickly learned and becomes a determined habit

BARN SOUR

If your horse refuses to leave the barn or other horses, take the reins about a foot apart. Keep the reins quite short; move your hands one third to halfway up the horse's neck, maintaining firm contact on the reins with the horse's mouth. The horse may attempt to wheel, and holding the reins in this manner makes it easier to prevent this. Then drive him forward energetically with legs, heels, spurs, or whip. Do not hesitate, and be very aggressive. Hit him forcefully with a whip behind your leg, and if he shows any tendency to hesitate once you have got him moving in the proper direction, *immediately* drive him forward again. Timing is the key to success; if you hesitate or show any indecision yourself, he will renew his resistance with increased determination. It is important to correct a barn-sour horse promptly because the next step is usually rearing, a much more serious vice.

Cause:

 ♦ The natural herd instinct in horses—a horse seldom wants to leave a group of other horses
 ♦ The desire to get back to the stall for feeding or rest
 ♦ A bad habit developed when the horse learns that by resistance he can do as he pleases

BEHIND THE BIT

If the horse refuses to meet the bit firmly and willingly, and tucks in his chin toward his chest to avoid maintaining contact with it, he is behind the bit. Use a mild bit, such as a thick hollow-mouth egg-butt snaffle or soft rubber straight-mouth snaffle (be sure that the rubber is not chipped and hardened or cracked). Do not use any bit that has a curb chain such as a Pelham or curb, as these tend to make a horse overbend to avoid the severe leverage action caused by the combined effects of the chain beneath the chin and the long shanks to which the reins are attached.

Behind the bit.

Trot and canter up and down rolling hills, since this encourages the horse to reach out with his head and neck for balance.

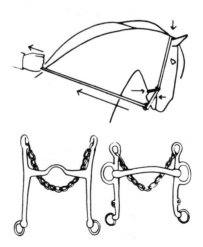

Top: Leverage action of *curb* and *Pelham* bits.

Bottom: Port-mouth curb bit, *half-moon Pelham* bit.

Ride at a trot over cavalletti (poles on the ground, six or eight in a row, about 3½ to 4 feet apart), which also encourages head and neck to reach out.

Do transitions from one gait to another (from walk to trot, walk to canter, and trot to canter, and vice versa) that encourage the horse to use his hind legs actively. A horse who travels behind the bit characteristically does not have much impulsion (energy from behind). Go only eight or ten steps in one gait before changing to another.

Use of cavalletti.

Work steadily at a trot on a circle, and as you do, encourage the horse to swing his hindquarters out by pushing him with your inside leg. This tends to make him take more positive contact with the bit, because when he moves his hind legs somewhat sideways (out on the circle) he automatically transfers some of his weight to the forehand. As the forehand receives more weight, the head and neck extend and lower, and the horse must therefore make firmer contact with the bit. When you have worked a few minutes in one direction, change the direction of the circle; when the horse works well on circles, begin to work on a serpentine (S-shaped turns in alternating directions).

Use a gentle soft pressure, being sure that you never accidentally yank him in the mouth. Keep the horse moving actively forward.

Some people find it useful to attach long, low side-reins (from snaffle rings to the girth, just below the bottom of the saddle flaps), as they are attached at both ends and therefore will remain perfectly steady, which may encourage the horse to maintain more positive contact with the bit. You can use side-reins when you longe your horse or when you ride. If you longe him, attach the longeline to a halter, not to the bit, since this would pull and hurt his mouth due to the weight of the longeline. If you ride, attach an extra set of reins from bit to girth, and use the other set in the normal way.

On the bit.

Cause:

- Pain or soreness in the mouth, due to injury by the bit or a tooth that has grown sharp. If you suspect this, have the teeth floated (filed by a specialist to remove overgrown sharp edges).
- Heavy-handed riding—rider gives a signal but fails to soften his hand when the signal has been obeyed.
- Bits with a curb chain. The pain caused by the leverage principle of the shank in combination with the action of the curb chain can be very great. Even a small pull of the reins causes a much greater action on the mouth and under the chin than the amount of pressure the rider exerts with his hands.
- Timidity—a horse who is fearful by nature does not willingly go forward with much boldness under any conditions.

BITING OTHER HORSES
WHILE BEING RIDDEN

Snatch the reins hard and sharply—backward and somewhat upward is more effective than straight back. If the horse breaks his gait or slows down, correct this immediately by giving the aids for the gait and rhythm you had before. A sharp word should accompany the snatch, such as "Hey, come up here!" (see Pinning Ears, page 86).

Cause:

- Although this is normal behavior for horses, it becomes unacceptable when they are being ridden, and if uncorrected becomes a vice.

Biting or kicking while ridden—snatching the reins.

"BLOWING UP"—INHALING AIR TO PREVENT GIRTH BEING MADE TOO TIGHT

This is one of the easiest problems of all to cure. When you put the saddle on your horse, fasten the girth very loosely—just tightly enough so the saddle will not fall off when the horse moves. When you are about to mount, draw up the girth a second time, and when you are in the saddle and have walked a minute or two, pull the girth up a third and final time (your weight pushing the saddle down will make it necessary to check even a girth that was tight enough when you mounted). In this way the horse will end up being girthed properly without any discomfort to him, and even a horse who "blows up" will eventually learn that there is no need to do so, since this method does not cause him pain or make him feel the need to protect himself. If you use an elastic-end girth you will find the problem quite a lot easier to deal with.

Never jab a knee or fist into a horse's side to force him to exhale his breath suddenly as you do up the girth. A horse mistreated in this way soon learns to defend himself by blowing up, or even by using his teeth and heels whenever he sees you coming with a saddle.

Cause:

- ♦ Mistreatment—a knee, fist, or elbow in the belly as horse is being saddled.
- ♦ Discomfort—a badly fitting saddle, which causes the horse to dread its being put on his back; or a dirty or badly fitted girth that rubs a sore spot on the horse's girth area.

BOLTING

Bolting is running at top speed, out of control, usually in a straight line. The horse is in a state of panic, not thinking of anything but running away from what he considers danger.

Raise your hands, first loosening the reins, then snatch back abruptly at the same time that you push your heels down and forward, as you would for Bucking (see page 40).

It is impossible to *out-pull* a bolting horse, but by giving a severe, abrupt snatch once or several times in a row, you can make the horse lift his head and front end slightly and shift his weight back somewhat (rather like a seesaw, one end going down as the other is elevated), and in this way stop him.

Be sure that you do not give a steady pull, but rather a hard snatch on the reins. This will be more effective if you let the reins become slightly slack for the split second before you snatch them.

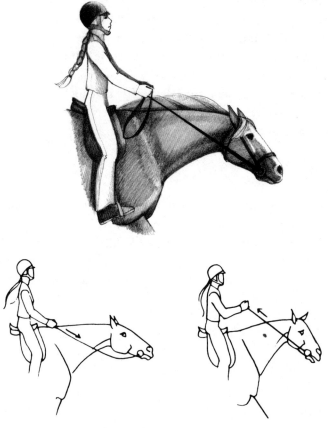

BOLTING.

Top: Incorrect—rider maintaining steady backward pull.

Lower left: Correct—release reins forward.

Lower right: Correct—snatch upward and backward.

Do not attempt to turn a bolting horse in a tight circle. In a very large field that has no holes underfoot, you could turn him gradually in a circle, but a bolting horse may fall if turned too sharply when running flat out or if the footing is poor.

ALPHABETICAL LISTING OF PROBLEMS

The long-term cure for bolting is reschooling. Use the same exercises—transitions—you would to reschool a horse who pulls (see Pulling, page 91).

A standing martingale, while not actually curing the problem, will make it easier to control a horse who is prone to bolt, as it prevents him from raising his head too high; therefore, when you snatch the reins he cannot attempt to escape the punishment by raising his head. Adjust the martingale strap so that it just meets the horse's throat when you push it upward with your hand when the horse's head is in a normal, relaxed position.

Adjusting a standing martingale.

NOTE: Some people recommend use of a *chambon*, also called a French martingale, for use on horses who habitually bolt. A snap attaches to the ring of the bit on each side, a piece of nylon cord goes from this snap through a ring attached to the bridle's crownpiece on each side and down to a point beneath the horse's throat, where both attach to a standing martingale that fastens to the girth in the normal way. Whenever the horse tries to raise his head to bolt, he gives himself a jab in the mouth and causes a strong pressure to be exerted on his poll by the crownpiece of the bridle. Use of the chambon can be risky, however, as some horses react violently to it and may rear up or even flip over. You should never attempt to ride a horse in a chambon until he has been thoroughly accustomed to it on a longeline with side-reins first. In any case, an educated rider using a standing martingale can accomplish the same result with less risk.

Chambon (used with an *egg-butt snaffle*).

Cause:

- ◆ Lack of proper schooling. A horse quickly learns he can avoid work by bolting if he once tries it and is not corrected.
- ◆ Cold wind, especially if the horse is clipped and has just come out of the stable.

- Too much grain could be a contributing factor.
- Shying, if uncorrected, can lead to bolting. If you allow the horse to go at a faster pace after shying at something—for instance, if you were working at a trot when he shied at something, and afterward you allowed him to canter—he may soon learn to bolt.
- Heavy-handed riding may cause an attempt to "run away" from it.

BRIDLING—REFUSAL TO OPEN MOUTH FOR BIT

This is easy to correct. First wiggle a finger gently in the bars of the horse's mouth—where he has no teeth, only gums—until he opens his mouth. Do this several times until he readily opens his mouth. Next, holding the bridle, stand beside the horse on his left side, facing the same direction as the horse. Hold the left cheekpiece of the bridle in the left hand, the right cheekpiece in the right. Your right hand will have to reach under the horse's jaw to position the bit so that it lightly touches his front teeth; however, make no attempt to force it into his mouth. Now reach across his nose with your right hand and grasp both cheekpieces with the right hand, keeping your palm down across his nose so that he cannot raise his head to avoid accepting the bit.

Rest the bit on the thumb and middle finger of your left hand. Stick your thumb into the corner of the horse's lip on the side near you and wiggle it until he opens his mouth. Then pull up gently with the right hand, holding the cheekpieces, and when the bit is well into his mouth, slip each ear through the crownpiece in the usual way. Be sure to smooth the mane and forelock beneath the bridle so there is no discomfort, and also be sure the bit is adjusted so it just wrinkles the corners of the mouth, and that the throatlatch and cavesson (nosepiece) are not too tight.

On very cold days warm the bit with your hands before putting it into the horse's mouth.

BRIDLING.

Refusal to open mouth for bit.

Cause:

- ♦ Rider forcing the bit roughly against the horse's teeth.
- ♦ The horse's greenness or lack of understanding of what is expected.

BRIDLING—THROWING HEAD
WHEN BRIDLE IS REMOVED

If there is a curb chain, undo it. Better still, use a snaffle that will come out of the horse's mouth easily. Have the horse in a stall where he cannot back up. Stand on his left beside his head, facing in the same direction. Place your left palm firmly across the horse's nose, about six inches above the nostrils (where the cavesson of a bridle would lie). With your right hand, reach under his throat and up to his right ear. Slip off the crownpiece of the bridle from his right ear and slide it forward. At this moment hold firmly down with your left hand as the horse will try to throw his head up. He may try to back up; go with him, not letting go of his nose with your left hand.

Removing the bridle.

When you have freed his right ear from the bridle with your right hand, move this hand down to the nose, and hold his nose down with the right hand instead of the left. Be sure not to let go of the bridle as you do this; have the cheekpieces in the right hand at the same time that you hold his nose down with that hand.

Now comes the most critical point. Reach up with your left hand and slip the crownpiece from the left ear. A bridle-shy horse will panic as soon as he feels the bit begin to slide down in his mouth, which will now happen. He may try to throw his head violently upward. Your right hand, across his nose, and your right arm, holding his head close to your body, prevent this. Hold his head down until he has spit out the bit completely, and then soothe and praise him, holding your hand low to feed him a tidbit, to help him see a connection between keeping his head low and a reward.

In extreme cases some people advise undoing the cheekpieces of the bridle, literally taking the bridle apart while the horse is wearing it. In any case, always hold the horse's head down with one hand (see Headshy, page 55).

Cause:

- ♦ Fear of pain, caused by a bad experience due to the rider's forgetting to unfasten a curb chain before removing the bridle. Unless the chain is unfastened the bit cannot come out of the mouth, and the horse throws his head up to try to escape the resulting jab of pain.
- ♦ An ignorant rider who punishes a frightened horse for throwing his head can aggravate the problem and frighten the horse to the point where he panics when even a snaffle is removed.

BUCKING

A horse can only buck if he can lower his head. If you prevent this, he cannot buck.

Lift the horse's head by a sharp, abrupt snatch on the reins. Take a full-cross on the reins (see illustration, page 92) and have them fairly short, so that you can give a very hard snatch. To accomplish this, as you feel the horse begin to lower his head in preparation to buck, move your hands toward his mouth for an instant before you snatch the reins; having the reins slightly slack

Bucking.

allows the snatch to be far more abrupt. The abruptness is important, because if you pull the reins too slowly, the horse can easily
outpull you. The key to success lies in making the snatch so
abrupt that he cannot react to it by pulling.

Your hands should move on a line from the horse's mouth
toward your own chest or chin, more or less (see illustration, page
32). Try to time the snatch so that the downward movement of
the horse's head as he bucks meets the back-and-upward snatch, as
this is the most effective moment.

At the same time, push your heels down and well forward,
and lean back so that you are not thrown forward by the combined effects of the horse putting his head down and raising his
back.

Cause:

- Cold weather, especially if it is windy and the horse has been clipped.
- Playfulness—spooking at objects that do not really frighten him, simply for the fun of it.
- Lack of exercise, especially if the horse is kept in a stall and not turned out long enough each day (see Longeing note, page 80).
- Too much grain could be a contributing factor.
- Pain caused by badly fitting tack or a burr or twig accidentally caught between saddle pad and horse's back. In rare cases internal pain, caused by a cracked vertebra, bruised rib, etc. If you suspect injury, do not ride and call a vet.

CANTER—DISUNITED

When a horse canters correctly the sequence of footfalls is as follows: first beat—outside hind leg; second beat—outside foreleg and inside hind leg moving at the same time; third beat—the inside leading foreleg. The three beats are followed by a moment of suspension in which all four legs are completely off the ground. See figures 1 to 4, page 43.

If the horse canters in any other manner, the canter is disunited and the horse must be brought to a walk or trot, whichever you were doing when you gave the signal to canter. You must then give the signal to canter again, clearly and immediately.

If you are not sure of the correct aids for the canter, see Canter—Refusal to Take or Keep Correct Lead, page 44.

The disunited canter is easy to recognize: It is usually rough and feels awkward, with the horse's body lurching somewhat sideways in a rolling motion with each stride. However, a good

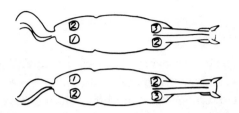

CANTER—CORRECT SEQUENCE OF FOOTFALLS.

Top: Left lead. *Center:* Right lead.

Bottom: Right lead (three beats plus a moment of suspension).

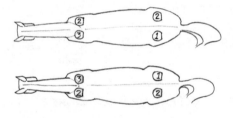

DISUNITED CANTER.

Top: Sequence of footfalls, left lead disunited.

Center: Sequence of footfalls, right lead disunited.

Bottom: Right lead disunited, first beat.

rider who can clearly recognize by feel the three beats of the correct canter will know exactly what the horse is doing with his feet: In disunited canter he steps off with his *inside* hind leg, followed by the outside hind leg and outside foreleg together, then the inside leading foreleg.

Cause:

- ♦ The rider asking for the canter at the wrong moment in the sequence of footfalls of the walk or trot
- ♦ The rider hurrying the horse into a canter with too abrupt or harsh a signal
- ♦ Possible lameness or unsoundness, making it painful for the horse to canter correctly

CANTER—
REFUSAL TO TAKE OR KEEP CORRECT LEAD

The signals for canter are: inside indirect rein and outside leg, each giving an active squeeze, while the other rein and leg remain relatively passive (see Canter—Disunited, page 42, for sequence of footfalls; and Indirect Rein, page 22).

To strike off on a canter on left lead use indirect left rein (that is, put gentle pressure on the left rein, moving your hand on a diagonal line that would cross the withers if you brought it back far enough, rather than moving it straight back). At the same time, squeeze with the opposite leg, in this case, your right leg, slightly behind the girth. As you do this, hold the right rein snugly enough so the horse cannot bend his neck to the left, which he will try to do when he feels the left indirect rein. Your hands should remain parallel—that is, move the right hand away from the neck a few inches. However, keep your touch on both reins as light as possible.

ALPHABETICAL LISTING OF PROBLEMS

Allow your left leg to lie normally against the horse's side unless it is needed to push the horse actively out on the circle if he tries to move sideways away from the action of your right leg.

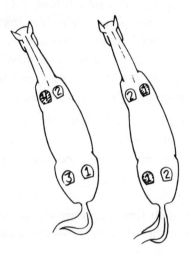

CANTER, LEFT LEAD.

Give signal when darkened foot or feet have just touched ground.
Left: From walk to canter.   *Right:* From trot to canter.

A horse is more inclined to take the correct lead if he is working on a circle about 25 or 30 feet in diameter rather than on a straight line, so in teaching leads always work on a circle, repeating the signal for canter several times in one direction before changing direction.

You must give the signal to canter at the precisely correct moment.

To go from a walk to canter on left lead, this moment is just as he points his inside (left) forefoot out and begins to touch it to the ground because this is the fourth and final beat of the walk, and the next beat (the right hind leg) must initiate the first beat of the canter. You must give the signal to canter during the last beat of the walk in order to instruct the outside (right) hind leg to begin the first step of the canter rather than another step of the walk.

To go from rising trot to canter on left lead, give the signal as you begin to sit down again after rising (posting) with the right diagonal (right fore and left hind), because at this moment the horse's right hind foot is in the air. You must instruct this foot before it hits the ground that its next step must be the first step of the canter rather than another step of the trot.

To go from sitting trot to canter (keep the trot slow or it will be too bumpy to sit), give the signal as the right diagonal (right fore and left hind) is on the ground and the outside hind foot is therefore in the air, as for rising trot.

If the horse fails to break into a canter and merely trots faster, steady him with firmer pressure on the reins and use your leg actively, or use the whip right behind your outside leg and give the signal to canter again.

To go from rising trot to canter, sometimes with young horses it helps to urge with your body as you rise to the trot on the outside diagonal, prolonging this upward beat by staying out of the saddle a fraction of a second longer than usual, then sitting a "short beat" to make up for the lost time.

If the horse breaks into a canter but quickly falls into a trot, he lacks impulsion, which you must create by increasing your driving (leg) aids without letting the horse go any faster. He must use the energy created by your legs to step farther under his body with his hind legs. To make him do this, put a light pressure on both reins while cantering, drive his hind legs under him with your legs, then soften your hands when you feel him become balanced and collected. You will feel this moment because his hind legs will be farther under his body, his front end will be slightly elevated, and he will no longer be pulling.

If the horse takes the incorrect lead even though you have given the correct signal, bring him immediately back to the gait

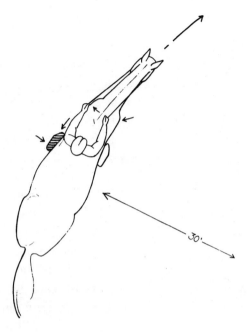

Canter—signals for right lead.

you had when you gave the signal. Wait for the proper moment, and give the signal again. Canter for fifteen or twenty strides, then reward the horse with a rest period at the walk on a long, loose rein.

If he changes leads (a flying change) without being asked or becomes disunited, immediately return to a trot and give the signal for the correct lead.

Cause:

- Improper schooling
- Greenness
- Persistent inability to remain on a certain lead may indicate soreness (pulled muscles or underdeveloped muscles) or unsoundness (chronic lameness due to injury or disease)

—— 47 ——

HORSE SENSE

CANTER—TOO FAST

Increase your leg aids to drive the horse's hind legs under him. At the same time, hold the reins with enough pressure to prevent the horse from using this increased energy to go faster.

When he shifts his center of gravity back (as his hind legs move under him) soften your hand (that is, move your hand forward or momentarily open your fingers, removing the pressure from the bit). If the horse raises his head, see Above the Bit—"Stargazing" on page 23.

The faster a horse canters, the more he tends to go on the forehand and the less he treads under his body with his hind legs. You must therefore shift his weight back—(like a seesaw, when the hind end comes down and under, the forehand is elevated). A horse cantering with his hocks well under his body canters more slowly and with more collection than a horse traveling on his forehand.

Do not be rough or abrupt in this exercise, and expect only small changes little by little. Otherwise you will destroy the free forward movement, and the horse in his attempt to escape a harsh hand will try serious evasions such as cantering sideways, turning his head to one side, or coming behind the bit.

Cause:

- ♦ Greenness—young horses tend to canter with head and neck carried low and extended; it is easier for them to canter fast than to canter slowly.
- ♦ Evasion—a horse learns that he can avoid work he does not like or understand by "running away" from it if the rider does not know how to correct this evasion.

CATCHING HORSE IN A FIELD

Keep a leather halter on your horse when he is turned out (a nylon halter does not break easily and could prove dangerous if the horse catches it on something). If possible, have the horse in a field of a half-acre or smaller, or adjacent to a paddock into which he can be lured or chased.

Take a bag of carrots and a leadshank and walk after your horse. Do not hurry; maintain a calm but purposeful walk. At first he will gallop madly from one end of the pasture to the other, stopping only to snort and stare defiantly at you before wheeling and taking off again. Continue to walk steadily after him. Presently he will begin to trot instead of gallop, and finally slow to a walk.

Always approach the horse's head. If he turns his hindquarters toward you, give them a wide berth and again approach him from the head.

When he finally stops and does not attempt to run away, make no sudden movements. Very gently, with as little movement as possible, snap the leadshank onto his halter and give him a tidbit.

The key is to continue going after the horse at a calm but persistent pace. The first time it may take as long as an hour (so allow plenty of time), the next time half an hour, and so on. But this method works with practically any horse.

When the horse realizes you will not give up nor become upset or impatient, but will merely pursue him relentlessly as long as he resists you, he will finally give up this tactic as a means of evading you.

NOTE: Some people suggest leaving a piece of rope about two feet long always attached to the halter to make it easier to catch a horse who is difficult to approach. The possible drawbacks of this are that the rope could get caught on something, the end could hit the horse's eye, or he could step on it while grazing and break his halter.

Cause:

- ◆ Lack of handling
- ◆ Fear of people as a result of mishandling
- ◆ High spirits

HORSE SENSE

Dogs—Lunging, Biting, or Kicking At

If a horse lowers his head toward a dog and pins his ears (flattens his ears back against his head) the next thing he will probably do is bite or kick the dog. Do not wait until he actually does so; correct him at the first sign of bad temper (see illustration, page 87).

Snatch the reins sharply and use a verbal command, such as those for Biting Other Horses While Being Ridden (see page 31).

If a horse attempts to back up and kick at a dog, use whip or spurs energetically to drive him forward. At the same time, keep his head up so he cannot buck (and kick at the dog simultaneously). It may help to introduce the horse while unmounted to a dog that is friendly; however, use caution so the dog is not attacked or bitten.

Cause:

- ◆ Bad temper, if uncorrected by the rider
- ◆ Fear—the horse may have been attacked or pursued by a dog

Ducking Out When Passing an Open Gate

This occurs most often while working in an outdoor ring. If you even suspect your horse may try this, carry your whip in the outside hand (the side nearest the open gate). At the first move he makes to duck out, slap his shoulder with the whip, keeping your hand on the outside rein, and kick hard once or twice with your heel on the same side. At the same time, pull his head toward the center of the ring with the inside rein, and keep him moving forward.

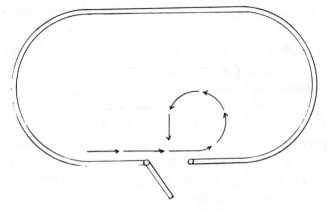

Correct exit from a ring through an open gate.

To prevent the problem from recurring, always do the following when preparing to leave the ring: Walk past the open exit, circle toward the middle of the ring, then walk straight out the gate on a long loose rein (free walk). If you have trouble making your horse free walk, see Jigging, page 56, and teach him that lesson first.

If you always exit in this manner the horse will learn that he may never slip out the gate when he is beside it but may only exit when he has circled and is approaching it head-on. In addition, he will learn not to attempt to exit while being ridden with the usual working rein contact, but only when on a long loose rein.

Cause:

♦ Natural inclination, if uncorrected by the rider

EATING WHILE BEING RIDDEN

This annoying habit can be cured fairly easily as long as the rider is absolutely consistent. Every time the horse makes a grab for a

mouthful of greenery, snatch the reins hard. If he actually man-
ages to get something into his mouth, pull it out before he can
chew or swallow it so that he never achieves his aim. If you never
let him eat while ridden, he will give up trying to grab at snacks
when you ride him.

But do not expect a horse to know when it is all right to eat
and when it is not; don't let him do it sometimes and at other
times punish him. It is not cruel to forbid him to eat while being
ridden, but it is cruel to give him conflicting rules that confuse
him, and to punish him for something that you previously allowed
him to do. Never let him eat "just this once."

If you are on a long ride and want to allow him some grass,
get off and graze him by hand with his bridle on (if you have no
halter). He will easily differentiate between grazing when you are
leading him and when you are riding him. Again, be consistent,
and realize that he will always want to be allowed to eat while you
are leading him if you sometimes allow it. It is better to put his
halter on before letting him eat, although in certain circumstances
this may not be practical.

Cause:

♦   The horse's natural inclination

FEET—REFUSAL TO PICK UP

To check a horse's feet for stones, to clean them with a hoof pick,
or to check the condition of his feet, you need to be able to pick
up his feet.

Be sure that the horse is in an enclosed area like a stall, or
that an assistant holds him for this exercise; otherwise he will
probably walk away.

To pick up the left front foot, stand beside the horse's left

Picking up feet.

shoulder, facing the tail. Run your left hand down the leg and over the fetlock joint. Lean with your left shoulder lightly against the horse's shoulder, which will help to shift his weight to the other foreleg and make him more inclined to pick up the foot next to you. Keep your left hand on the pastern while you pinch the back part of the fetlock with your right hand. When the horse picks up the foot, hold it up by the pastern for only a second or two, then put it down and praise him. It is best to repeat the exercise several times, gradually increasing the length of time you hold the foot off the ground. If you try to hold it up too long at first, you run the risk of his setting it down in spite of your efforts to hold it up.

If the horse absolutely refuses to lift his foot, very gently tap the hoof or pastern with the toe of your boot, being ready to catch the pastern and hold it up the moment the hoof leaves the ground, which will happen very suddenly. As before, hold his foot up by the pastern only a moment at first, gradually lengthening the time as you repeat the exercise.

HORSE SENSE

Cause:

- Horse lacks proper education.
- *Fear.* A person may have punished him with rough handling when he did not understand what was expected.

HALT—REFUSAL TO STAND SQUARELY

WHEN LEADING. As you lead the horse, watch the position of his feet. Try to stop at the moment he will stop with all four feet positioned squarely; if one leg is trailing behind, tap it gently with a whip or the toe of your boot, just hard enough to make him move that foot into position. Stand for several seconds, and repeat. If he tries to move a foot without being asked to, shake gently on the leadshank or the reins and say "Ho!" (not loudly, but distinctly). Always use this word to mean only a *complete* halt, never to mean "slow down."

WHEN RIDING. *To go from walk to halt,* use the same procedure as when leading, having an assistant tap the horse's feet if necessary to obtain a square halt.

To go from trot to halt, say "Ho!" as you give the signal to halt (squeeze with both legs to push the horse's hind legs under him, and at the same time put pressure evenly on both reins until he comes to a complete halt; then soften your hand and discontinue your leg aids). Make sure the horse does not move at all after he has halted, even if one leg is trailing behind him. If he tries to move that leg to make it even with the other, snatch the reins and repeat "Ho!" quietly but firmly. The key is to make him realize that once he has come to a halt, he will be made to stand absolutely still, no matter how awkwardly he has placed his legs. If he has not halted squarely he will have to stand still in that uncomfortable position for a long time (count to twenty before you allow the horse to move off into a walk), so he will find it to his advantage to halt squarely.

To go from canter to halt, use the same procedure as from trot to halt.

The reason the procedure differs for the two faster gaits from that for the walk is because at the trot or canter there is much more chance that the horse will halt with a sprawled-out stance, and it will be awkward for him to remain so; at the walk he has more control over his halt and will probably halt in a more comfortable position, although not necessarily in a perfectly square halt.

Cause:

- ♦ Horse being allowed to move after coming to a halt, thereby adjusting his position when it suits him instead of halting squarely in the first place
- ♦ Lack of education

HEADSHY

If your horse raises his head abruptly or ducks away from you whenever you try to touch his head or ears, he is headshy. This problem is caused by fear, and you must therefore not punish him. Instead, be patient and gentle, and be aware that although the cure will take time, it is possible to reeducate headshy horses successfully.

Have him in a stall so that he cannot run away. Gently rub the horse's neck, feeding him a tidbit and talking quietly to him. Gradually move your hand toward his lower jaw; when he will allow you to rub there, rub up toward his ears. *Never grab an ear and hold onto it.* If he becomes frightened and raises his head, let him; when he has calmed down, begin again. The key is patience. It may take weeks or months before he will trust you.

HORSE SENSE

In an extreme case where the horse is so fearful of having his ears touched that you cannot put a bridle on him, you should first try the above method of reeducating him. In an emergency, however, you can sometimes bridle a headshy horse by taking the bridle apart where the cheekpiece buckles onto the crownpiece, placing each part where it belongs, and rebuckling it, thus avoiding the problem of having to touch his ears. But with a terrified horse this can be dangerous, as you may get pinned against the wall or stepped on in his panic.

Cause:

♦ Cruel and improper handling such as a twitch having been used on a horse's ear (a twitch is a loop of rope or chain on the end of a stick in which the lip is twisted until pain distracts the horse from reacting to the fact he is being shod, having his teeth floated, or undergoing anything else he finds unpleasant).

♦ A person striking the horse on the head with a whip or heavy object.

♦ A rider failing to hold the horse's head down when unbridling him, the bit getting caught in the horse's mouth when he raises his head (see Bridling—Throwing Head When Bridle Is Removed, page 38).

♦ Very green young horses may show some signs of headshyness until they have grown accustomed to being handled.

JIGGING—REFUSAL TO WALK
(A SHORT-STRIDING TROT, USUALLY WITH THE HORSE'S HEAD ABOVE THE BIT)

If your horse jigs when you are teaching him difficult new work (when a young horse is first taught walk-to-canter transitions, for example), simply bring him as calmly into a walk as you can, and continue with the work. In such cases, jigging is caused by anxiety because the horse knows he is about to be given a signal he does not yet fully understand. In this case, the jigging will disappear as soon as he learns what the signal means. Too severe a correction would upset him and impede the lesson's progress, so it is best to correct the jigging with a minimum amount of fuss.

But if the horse has learned to jig as a habit—some short-legged horses jig when ridden in the company of longer-striding ones—or if the horse is simply keyed-up and excited, as when hunting, for instance—then correct him with the following method:

Hold the buckle of the reins with your right hand. Keep this hand just above the withers so that the horse has the full length of reins and can extend his head fully without making contact with the bit. At the same time, keep the left hand loosely closed around the reins just in front of your right hand. As long as the horse walks quietly, do nothing. But at the first jigging step, pull back sharply with the right hand on the buckle. Your left hand remains in place just in front of the withers as the reins slide

Jigging—shortening the reins to give a light snatch.

through your lightly closed left fingers (see illustration, page 57).
Give a light snatch on the reins, just hard enough to make the
horse stop jigging and walk a four-beat walk. Then immediately
give him the full rein as before. Repeat every time he jigs, until he
learns not to attempt it. He will soon see that it is to his
advantage not to, since he will prefer to walk with his head
comfortably extended rather than earn a snatch each time he jigs.
Next teach the horse to lower and extend his head and neck (see
Above the Bit—"Stargazing," page 23), since a horse with low
head carriage will not jig.

Cause:

♦ Anticipation—horses learning new work sometimes jig
when they know they are about to be asked to do something they do not fully understand
♦ Eagerness to return to the barn after a ride
♦ Excitement of any kind
♦ A short-legged horse attempting to keep up with a longer-
striding one

JUMPING—DANGLING LEGS
OVER THE FENCE
(FAILURE TO "FOLD")

The best way for a horse to jump a fence is to clear the fence by
as little as possible. That is, both his front feet and hind feet
should be not more than 2 or 3 inches above the fence as he
jumps it; thus his body will clear the fence by no more than a few
inches. The more the horse "folds" (bends his knees and tucks his
front legs up close to his body, and pulls his hind legs up as high
as possible over the fence), the less effort the horse must make in
order to jump the fence: A horse who folds well does not need to

hoist his body as high into the air to get over the fence as a horse who dangles his legs (see illustration, page 63).

It is therefore important to encourage your horse to fold when he jumps. Some horses do it naturally, others need to be encouraged to do so.

Have someone else jump the horse over three or four straight fences of varying heights—from 2 feet to 3½ feet in height. Do not use a ground-line (a pole laid on the ground a foot or two in front of the jump that helps the horse to judge his take-off point correctly); that is, give the horse every chance to "make a mistake" if he is inclined to jump badly. Watch him from the side, so that you can see whether he *bascules* (see Failure to Bascule, page 60). Pay particular attention to whether he jumps by picking up his knees and feet, tucking them up close to his body as he goes over the fence, or whether he dangles his legs, thereby making it necessary for him to lift his body high into the air as he jumps. If he dangles his legs, do the following exercises:

BUILD A JUMPING LANE (see pages 71–73). Let your horse jump these without a rider. Note whether he jumps better over smaller or larger fences (some horses will fold over large fences but won't bother over small ones) and whether he dangles his legs over straight upright fences but jumps spread fences well, and so forth. Whichever fences he jumps badly, you will ride him over in the next exercise.

RIDE OVER FENCES THE HORSE FINDS DIFFICULT. Build five or six fences of the type the horse jumps least well. Practice riding over them until he is comfortable with them. In some cases, simply getting a horse used to something he finds difficult will improve his jumping style.

RIDE OVER SOLID SPREAD FENCES such as a pile of telephone poles, two or more at the bottom, one or more on top, in a triangular formation (see illustration, page 72), barrels on their sides with a ground-line, chicken coops, and so on. Horses tend to fold better over solid fences that don't knock down as easily as can a pole on jump standards (holders).

HAVE AN ASSISTANT RIDE THE HORSE OVER AN UPRIGHT FENCE WITH A BAMBOO POLE LAID ALONG THE TOP OF IT. As the horse jumps the fence, sharply raise the bamboo pole and hit his front legs or feet. Try to hit between the coronet and knee on the cannon bone; be sure that you do not hit his knees or higher than his knees. The purpose is to make him lift his feet and fold his legs over the fence. The pole should be long enough so you can hit the horse accurately as he jumps even if he jumps to one side of the fence, but not so long as to be unwieldy to handle. If possible, have a second assistant hold the other end of the pole and help to strike the horse's cannon bone with it as he jumps.

Cause:

- ◆ Lack of natural jumping ability caused by poor conformation
- ◆ Carelessness—some horses find small fences too boring to jump well and only fold over larger fences
- ◆ Unfamiliarity with a certain type of fence, causing the horse to rush the fence or jump it badly in a panic

JUMPING—"FLAT"
(FAILURE TO BASCULE)

Failure by the horse to round his back and neck and "use himself" over a fence is called jumping "flat" or failure to bascule.

To a certain extent a horse's jumping style is determined by his conformation and natural ability or lack of it. But there are exercises that will help develop his judgment and athletic ability and that will improve his style of jumping.

ALPHABETICAL LISTING OF PROBLEMS

First, construct an upright fence 2½ feet high, and place a ground-line (a solid pole that is easy to see) on the landing side rather than on the take-off side. Put the pole the same distance from the fence as the fence is high—that is, 2½ feet from it—and jump this a few times, first at the trot, then at the canter.

Next, roll the pole away from the fence another few inches, until it is perhaps 3 feet from the fence. The horse will learn to expect a pole on the landing side of the fence and realize that he must therefore stay in the air longer in order to clear both the fence and the pole. This encourages him to "use himself" (bascule) over the fence, because a horse jumping in a short, choppy, up-down movement will not be able to clear the pole on the landing side.

Next, construct a one-stride in-and-out consisting of two vertical fences 2½ feet high and about 20 feet apart (more or less, according to the size of your horse). Place a ground-line on the landing side of the first element of the in-and-out and on the take-off side of the second element. Place those two ground-lines 3 feet from the fences—that is, slightly farther from the fences than the fences are high. The effect of the in-and-out is to cause the horse not only to use himself over the first element but to fit a

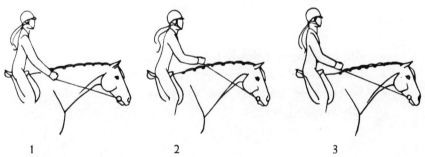

1   2   3

JUMPING—POSITION OF HANDS.

1. Incorrect—hands below straight line.

2. Correct—hands above straight line.

3. Correct—hands on straight line.

shorter stride in the middle, which makes him shift his weight back on his hocks, thereby giving his front end ample time to get off the ground before encountering the second element.

Cause:

- ♦ Greenness, lack of schooling
- ♦ Conformation faults—horses with long backs and short necks, for example

JUMPING—"GETTING UNDER" THE FENCE
(TAKE-OFF TOO CLOSE)

If the horse consistently "gets under" his fences, you may be approaching too slowly for the size of the fence. However, if a change in speed does not correct the problem, use the exercises described in Jumping—"Standing Back" Too Far, page 71, and in Jumping—"Flat," page 60.

If a normally good jumper suddenly jumps "short," it is probably due to soreness; have a vet check him before further work.

Cause:

- ♦ Approaching too slowly for size of fence
- ♦ Greenness—lack of ability to judge distance
- ♦ Soreness or lameness due to injury or a horseshoe nail driven too close

JUMPING—RUNNING OUT OR STOPPING

Never ride a horse toward a fence unless you are sure he can jump it. Take into account the fence's approach: Is it muddy or icy and therefore slippery? What is the horse's experience and level of

Top: Incorrect—Horse jumps without folding legs and must expend extra effort to clear fence.

Bottom: Correct—Horse folds legs correctly and clears fence with minimum effort.

training? Even if he is physically able to jump a particular fence, is it a great deal bigger and very different in appearance from what he has been used to? When in doubt, don't jump. If the horse is green and inexperienced, jump only small, easy obstacles and gradually increase their size and difficulty as he gains experience. In the case of bad approaches like ice or mud, if you *must* jump (for instance, out hunting when there is no way around a fence) set the fence as low as possible and try to follow another horse over to give your horse confidence. If you follow another horse stay two lengths behind him; this is close enough to encourage your horse to follow, but not so close that he attempts to take off at the same moment as his leader, which can be disastrous if he is one half-length behind the leading horse.

If you are sure the horse can jump a fence, ride him toward it with energy and a steady, sure approach. If you feel him slow down or waver as he approaches the fence, immediately correct this: Drive him forward with both legs and whip if necessary, and at the same time hold your reins 10 inches or more apart to minimize the chance of his running out to the side.

If, despite a good approach, the horse stops abruptly at the last moment, do not let him turn away from the fence. Back him two or three horse lengths, and, while he is facing the fence, hold the reins firmly enough so that he will not lunge suddenly forward, and then punish him with two or three sharp strokes of the whip. If the horse tried to run out to the right-hand side of the fence, hit him on the right, and vice versa. Use the whip just behind your leg. If you hold it so the major portion of it is inverted in your hand and is sticking up in the air instead of

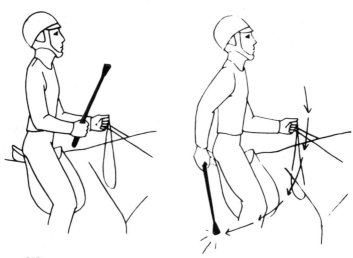

USE OF WHIP.

Left: Holding whip inverted for maximum effectiveness.

Right: Using whip correctly just behind rider's leg.

hanging down, you will be able to hit much more effectively than if you hold it in the usual way (see illustration, page 64).

There may be a time when a horse cannot jump a fence he has refused unless you circle and come at it a second time, such as in a group, where the horses following would run over you if you backed your horse from the fence. But in general, avoid circling as it takes more time; you should correct the refusal as soon as possible after it occurs. Also, the longer the new approach, the more time the horse has to think up new ways of avoiding jumping the fence a second time. Quick, energetic correction is the key.

Cause:

- ◆ The rider asking a horse to jump a fence with a bad approach, or one that is too difficult for his level of training and experience
- ◆ Curiosity on the horse's part as to what will happen if he stops or runs out
- ◆ In rare cases, pain (if you suspect this, do not ride, call a vet)

JUMPING—RUSHING

Rushing is approaching a fence too fast, often at least slightly out of control.

Be sure that your horse has thoroughly learned the lesson for standing still on command (if not, see Leading—Bolting, page 76).

Set up a low jump, not more than a foot high. Walk the horse toward the jump, approaching on a straight line. When you are about 20 feet from the jump, stop and stand still. Be sure you release the reins; that is, have no pressure on them after the horse stops, and make him stand without your holding him with the reins. If he moves, lightly snatch the reins and say "Ho!"

Now approach the jump without any backward rein pressure at all (you may need to take one rein to the side, away from his neck, to keep the horse heading straight toward the jump, but be sure you do not pull backward at all). If he will walk, well and good; however, even if he gallops the 20 feet do not interfere with him at all; let him do whatever he wants (except try to run out to one side, in which case use direct rein to keep him heading straight).

The moment he has jumped the fence, halt him abruptly on the *far* side of the fence. To do this, raise your hands somewhat at the same time you bring them backward. Your hands will move in a direction more or less toward your chin (see illustration, page 32). Say "Ho!" whenever you ask for a complete halt.

The horse will learn that there is no point in rushing since he always has to stop on the far side of the fence anyway. When he halts easily use less and less rein to stop him, just a little "bump" on the rein, and the verbal command.

Most important, the horse will gain confidence and be less inclined to rush due to fear, because you never attempt to interfere with his mouth as he approaches the fence. When he learns that there will always be a 20-foot approach zone in which he will have freedom to extend his head and neck to judge the distance to take off and to bascule (round his back and neck and "use himself"

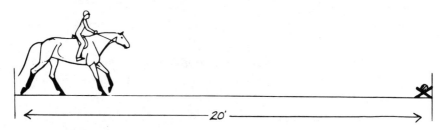

JUMPING—RUSHING FENCES.

A 20-foot zone of noninterference before the jump.

over the fence), the major cause of rushing in the first place—fear of interference by the rider—will have been removed.

When the horse will jump quietly from a walk, do this exercise from a trot, and finally from a canter. If he hurries at any point up *until* you reach the 20-foot zone, stop him, and then proceed. But be sure you stop him *prior* to the 20-foot zone, and leave him strictly alone after that until he has jumped the fence. If you interfere with his mouth too close before the fence, you may teach him to refuse to jump at all or make him panic because he feels he cannot negotiate the fence properly.

When the horse jumps calmly, omit the stop before the fence or the stop after it, or both. If he shows any signs of hurrying, repeat the halts as before.

Only raise the fence when he will jump it from both trot and canter without rushing or trying to break into a faster gait.

Another useful schooling exercise for the horse who rushes is this: First, lay a single pole on the ground. Trot toward it. As long as the horse remains perfectly calm, trot over the pole. If he shows any signs of rushing or pulling, turn away before the pole (you can get as close as one stride away if need be) and make a circle about 25 feet across, then approach the pole on the ground again. If he again rushes, again circle, this time the other way (alternate left and right, occasionally going twice in the same direction so he will never know which way he will be circled). The horse is never allowed to trot over the pole until he makes a perfectly calm approach; you may have to circle many times before the horse makes a good approach. Only raise the pole when he will go over it without rushing.

When he will trot quietly over the single pole on the ground, place four parallel poles (cavalletti) on the ground one trotting stride apart (the poles will be about 3½ to 4 feet apart, depending on the size of the horse) and repeat the exercise. As before, if the horse shows any sign of hurrying, turn away before the first pole and circle. Finally, remove the cavalletti and jump the small fence alone.

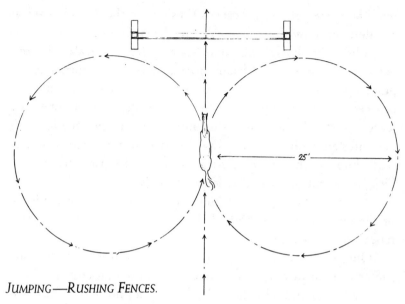

JUMPING—RUSHING FENCES.

Turn off before fence in alternate circles to left and right.

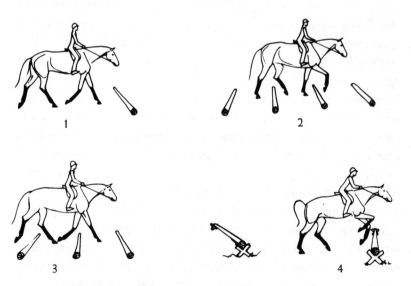

JUMPING—RUSHING FENCES.

Four steps in reschooling using cavalletti.

Next, set up a small fence 1½ feet high in place of the last cavalletto and repeat.

When he will jump the cavalletti and small fence quietly from a trot, place four or five small fences in a row, varying from about 9 feet to 12 feet apart, and trot over them. Change the distances slightly, so that the horse must pay attention to the spaces between fences and not merely assume that every two fences are the same distance apart. By keeping the fences low, under 2 feet high, you remove one of the main reasons for rushing—the horse being overfaced and expected to jump something he isn't sure he can— and you force him to pay attention to distances before and between fences—when he can judge distances well, he can arrive at the best spot for takeoff, and thus jump with much more ease and efficiency.

Next, set up a course of four or five fences scattered about, both single and combination fences, and jump each from several different angles. Work from a trot, and at the first sign of rushing, circle before the fence and approach again.

The key is persistence. Never jump any fence unless the horse has made a calm and steady approach. Expect a badly spoiled horse, or a horse excitable by nature, to require perhaps ten or fifteen circles before every fence jumped. If you find that even repeated circles fail to result in a calm approach, go back to the previous exercise, or even start right at the beginning again with a single pole on the ground. When the horse learns that jumping is a rather boring exercise consisting of endless circles as well as going over fences, he will become calm, finally, even if his experience with jumping has previously been of an exciting and agitating nature.

Cause:

♦ Some horses are excitable by nature, and want to rush.
♦ The rider interfering with the horse's mouth before a fence causes the horse to fear he will not be free to use his

head, neck, and back to get over the fence properly. (Consider the difficulty if you yourself were trying to jump a ditch while carrying another person piggyback, and at the last moment before you jumped, the person put his hands on your forehead and jerked your head backward.)

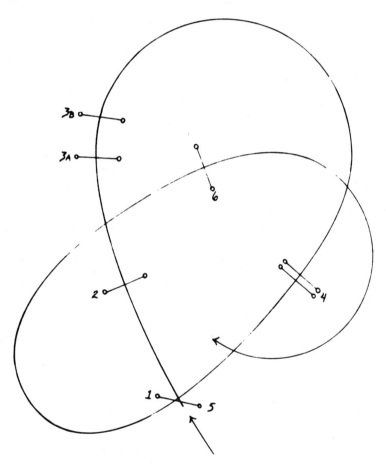

JUMPING—RUSHING FENCES.

A course of jumps using single uprights, combinations, fences jumped at an angle, and spread fences.

ALPHABETICAL LISTING OF PROBLEMS

◆ Pain from ill-fitting tack, which hurts more during the strain of jumping, or bad shoeing, lameness, or sore muscles. The horse seeks to run away from pain. Don't jump; call a vet.

◆ The horse being asked to jump too big or too difficult a fence for his level of training and development. Knowing the job is beyond his ability, he tries to run away from the problem by rushing.

JUMPING—"STANDING BACK" TOO FAR
(TAKEOFF TOO FAR FROM FENCE)

If the horse consistently "stands back" too far, you may be approaching too fast for the size of the fence. If you have trouble regulating the horse's speed as you approach the fence, see corrections for Jumping—Rushing, page 65. However, if a change in speed of approach does not correct the problem, the following schooling exercises will educate the horse to judge his distances more carefully.

First build a "jumping lane"—a series of four or five fences 1½ to 2 feet high (see illustration, page 72). Make them regularly spaced to fit your horse's canter stride (about 10 to 12 feet for a 15-hand horse going at medium speed). Make the fences as solid as possible so they will not knock down easily if the horse hits them; he must learn to respect fences as objects to be jumped cleanly, not crashed through if he misjudges his distance. He will land and take off immediately—a "no stride" or "bounce" stride— with no chance of taking off too far back.

Canter over the obstacles with as little rein as possible (keep the horse straight, but do nothing to interfere with forward movement) and let him make up his own mind as to where he wants to take off. If you see that you have made the jumps too close or too far apart for his stride, adjust them. When the horse can jump through the lane with a comfortable "no-stride" jump stride, repeat ten times or so.

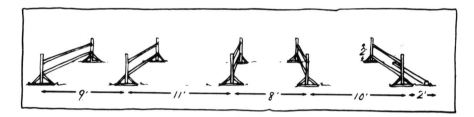

 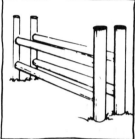 

JUMPING.

Top: "Jumping lane"—a row of "no-stride" fences set at varying distances apart. *Bottom:* Spread jumps.

Next make the spaces between the jumps irregular—that is, the first space 9 feet, the second 11 feet, the third 12 feet, for example. Ride through the lane as before, until the horse learns to adjust his stride himself.

Then change the spacing to a series of one-stride fences. Make these an average of 20 feet apart, a foot or two more or less either way for variation.

A second exercise that will help is to place a ground-line (a solid pole that is easy to see) on the ground in front of an upright fence. The ground-line should be the same distance in front of the fence as the fence is high—for a 2-foot jump, place the ground-line 2 feet in front of the jump. The horse tends to focus on the ground-line and pay attention to his take-off point.

A third exercise is to jump spread jumps and hogsback jumps—

four oil drums laid end-to-end on their sides are good, held in place by a long pole behind them; or a solid cinder-block wall with a pole above it; or three telephone poles in a triangular stack (two on the bottom and one on top). Such fences are a good schooling device because the horse must do two things: First, he cannot creep up to the fence and pop over it at the last minute because he would not have enough momentum to get completely over it; second, he cannot stand back too far and take off too early, as he would land right in the middle of the fence if he did, due to the width of its spread.

Cause:

- ♦ Approaching too fast for size of fence
- ♦ Greenness, lack of schooling

KICKING IN PASTURE

When a horse is loose in a field there is little you can do to prevent his kicking at other horses; this is normal behavior for horses until the "pecking order" is established. Once the herd has determined which horse is the "boss," which is "number two" and so on, there will be little or no kicking unless a new horse is introduced into the field, whereupon the newcomer must establish his place.

If a horse kicks repeatedly, his hind shoes can be removed so there is less chance of his injuring other horses. Or you could separate horses into small paddocks, although they seem happier when allowed to establish order together in their normal instinctive way.

Cause:

- ♦ Normal herd behavior of horses to establish "pecking order"

HORSE SENSE

KICKING OTHER HORSES WHILE BEING RIDDEN

Snatch the reins sharply and use a verbal command, as for Biting Other Horses While Being Ridden, page 31.

Do not use a whip or spurs on a horse who shows a tendency to kick at other horses; they will usually make a kicker lash out even more energetically.

Cause:

♦ Although normal behavior for horses, it is unacceptable while they are being ridden and if uncorrected becomes a vice

LEADING—BALKING

Lead your horse in a halter with a leather leadshank. (See illustrations, pages 75 and 76). Be sure to lead the horse properly, standing at his side beside his left shoulder, facing the same direction as the horse. Have an assistant with a long whip (a dressage whip is good) give the horse a sharp tap on his hindquarters from behind. If you must work alone, hold the lead in your left hand, the whip in your right. Be careful that the horse does not run over you when he reacts to the whip—be ready to move forward with him and also to steady him if he attempts to rush forward too quickly.

A verbal command will help the horse know that you want him to move forward when you are leading him. If you were riding, you could use your leg to give the command to go forward, but when leading from the ground it may not be clear, especially to a young or green horse, that you want him to step forward. Say in a confident tone something like "Come along."

Under no circumstances ever try to *pull* a horse forward; he will resist. Always drive a horse forward from behind with a whip.

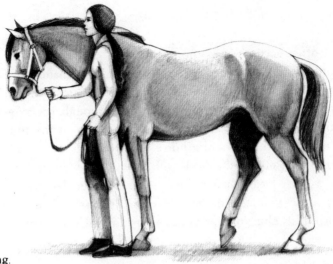

Leading.

NOTE: If you are alone and there is no one to assist you, an emergency measure that may help is to turn the horse's head to one side or the other, and pull the horse's head sideways so that he must either take a step or lose his balance. This will sometimes work well enough that a balky horse will forget his reluctance to move and will follow you once you get him moving. But any horse who balks habitually should be schooled not to do it, and the method with the whip is the only real way of impressing on him that he must not resist in this way.

Cause:

- Fear of danger—the horse approaches an object that frightens him.
- Curiosity—simply wondering what will happen if he resists. This behavior quickly becomes a bad habit if uncorrected.
- The horse, having been led improperly without a lead shank, learns that he can get away with balking.

HORSE SENSE

LEADING—BOLTING

This often occurs when a horse is being led through a gate or stall door. Use a leather leadshank with a one-foot chain end. Slip the chain through the ring on the left side of the halter near the muzzle, pass it under the horse's chin, through the ring on the right side of the muzzle, and attach the snap to the ring by the right cheek. If you have a horse who regularly bolts while being led, always attach the leadshank in this way. Never attempt to lead a horse by the halter alone, since if he decides to bolt there is very little you can do to prevent it unless you have a chain beneath his chin to impress upon him that he must stop.

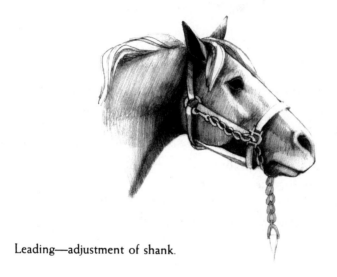

Leading—adjustment of shank.

Reeducate the horse under calm circumstances in a place where he cannot bolt, such as a ring or paddock.

To stop the horse, snatch the leadshank sharply downward and say at the same time "Ho!" He will lift his head abruptly and stop. Do not snatch so hard that he rears, but be fairly severe so he learns that the command word must be obeyed and there will be pain as long as he continues to go forward after he hears the word. If he moves again before you lead him forward, repeat as before. Keep your voice clear but not loud; rely on the sharpness of the snatch, not the loudness of your voice. As he responds better, use only a gentle tug to replace the snatch, and continue to use the verbal command.

When he understands the command well, practice the exercise in places where he normally would be reluctant to stop—just before an open gateway, just after, halfway through, or on very uneven ground, but be sure he doesn't panic and crowd you against the gateway. If the horse attempts to bolt, or even to take a single step after you have told him to stop, snatch several times in rapid succession, and repeat the verbal command.

NOTE: When you are ready to turn him loose, before you unsnap the leadshank always turn him to face the gate he has just come through. Never encourage him to gallop away when you unsnap the leadshank, but rather move quietly away from the horse yourself. Never wrap the leadshank around your hand. If a horse bolts you could get dragged.

Cause:

- ♦ The horse may have hit his hip bone when being led through a gate or stable doorway, and fear of pain makes him rush through
- ♦ The horse having been turned loose improperly after going through a gate

LENGTHEN STRIDE, REFUSAL TO

If a horse has a short, choppy stride at the walk, trot, or canter, first teach him to lengthen at the trot, because this even, two-beat gait is easier to control and you can most easily recognize when you have obtained a good, regular rhythm.

Extending the length of stride at a trot—the first step toward an "extended" trot—requires coordination of two signals. First, drive the horse actively forward with leg (and whip if needed). Second, do not allow the horse to use this increased forward energy to canter. To prevent this, first place a soft, even, smooth pressure on both reins equally, causing the horse to take a more positive hold than usual; then use your seat by posting with somewhat exaggerated emphasis.

If the horse becomes agitated and only takes faster trotting steps but with a very short stride that he refuses to lengthen, do not worry; push him on as fast as he will go. He will reach his limit, a point at which he cannot move his legs any faster. If you still continue to demand that he increase the energy he exerts by driving him forward, he will try to answer your demand in one of two ways, either by trying to break into a canter, or by lengthening stride.

If he canters, break the canter up by a "bump" on the reins—that is, release the reins just enough so that there is no pressure on them, then give a soft tug backward on both reins equally, something like a snatch, though not as hard.

Continue to post in the same rhythm you had when he was trotting. Do not make the canter easy for him by sitting to it in the usual way; your continuing to post even though he is cantering will make it awkward for him to canter and he will be more comfortable dropping back into a trot. When he trots again, push him on as before.

As you trot, post with a very definite rhythm. Exaggerate the up-down movement somewhat, and also slow down the rate of posting relative to the horse's trot. If he takes short, choppy strides very rapidly, post slightly slower than he is trotting, staying in the air a fraction of a second longer than you normally would.

When the horse has taken a few steps of trot with a longer

TROT.

Top: Incorrect—short, choppy stride.

Bottom: Correct—lengthening the stride.

stride than normal, use rein and leg to bring him back into an ordinary trot, so that the difference between the two lengths of stride will become clear to him. Do not expect too much too quickly; five or six steps showing just a little extension is enough at first. If you try for too much too quickly, he will become confused.

To teach a horse to lengthen stride at the walk, encourage him to move actively forward with legs and whip, if necessary. If he jigs when you do this, see correction for Jigging—Refusal to Walk, page 56.

To lengthen stride at the canter, work along a straight fence or wall to encourage straightness. Riding in company may encourage a horse who is not bold to move out and take longer strides.

Cause:

- ◆ Greenness, lack of schooling
- ◆ Excitement
- ◆ Conformation—a horse with little springiness or elevation and elasticity in his stride due to conformation faults (like short pasterns, straight shoulders, or high hocks) has little time off the ground in which to lengthen stride
- ◆ Unsoundness (lameness) or soreness

LONGEING—REFUSAL TO STAY OUT ON CIRCLE

Work in an enclosed area, ring, or paddock.

To work on a circle to the left, hold the longeline in your left hand and the whip in your right. The line should be attached to the horse's halter, not to a bit, as this would pull and hurt his mouth due to the weight of the line.

Start the horse out on a circle to the left, beginning with a small circle and gradually paying out the line to a length of about 20 feet. Hold the excess part of the longeline folded back on itself, never wrapped or looped around your hand; if the horse bolts you could get dragged.

To keep the horse out on the circle, "hold him" between the leading hand and the whip—that is, keep the whip normally behind the center of the horse, driving him actively forward, but if he begins to cut into the circle, point the whip toward his shoulder, and shake it at him to move him out on the circle again (see illustration, page 81).

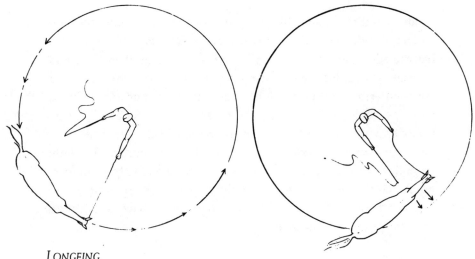

LONGEING.

Left: Increasing the pace or going into a faster gait.

Right: Moving the horse out on a circle.

The importance of voice commands is emphasized: Use the commands "walk," "trrrrot," and "canterrrrr" whenever you ask the horse to move forward at these gaits, and make the words sound as unalike as possible.

To halt, use the command "Ho!" and give a light tug on the longeline, at the same time pointing the whip at the horse's head or a few feet in front of him.

When you have halted the horse, *go to him, and do not bring him to you,* for that would encourage him to cut in on the circle.

Be aware that the faster you work the horse—at trot or canter—the larger a circle he must work on. Do not ask him to move at fast speeds on a tight circle because this could cause the horse to damage his legs or fall.

NOTE: As an alternative to longeing to "get the kinks out" of a high-spirited horse before you ride, turn him loose in a small paddock and chase after him flapping your hands, making him run around and do his exuberant bucks before you tack him up. This has the advantage of the horse's using more energy than he would on a longe and his having better control over what he does in a confined area and thus being less likely to injure himself. There is also a psychological benefit: If the horse is free to act as silly as he wants to before you ride him, he will be less likely to act this way under tack. When you are done chasing him around, speak calmly to him and make your own behavior very different from before; horses quickly understand when things are back to normal and will not confuse the two situations. It helps to have a carrot to offer when you are finished.

Cause:

♦ Greenness, lack of education
♦ Person allowing a horse to come into the circle prior to halting, or changing direction on a longeline rather than going to the horse

MOUNTING—REFUSAL TO STAND STILL

Work in an enclosed area such as a ring or paddock. The horse should be wearing a snaffle bit. Follow the procedure given for Leading—Bolting, page 76. When that lesson has been thoroughly learned, do the following:

Have an assistant stand at the horse's head, facing him, holding both reins, one in each hand. The reins will be in the normal position as for riding, but must be loose enough so that the assistant has most of the slack and can keep control of the horse. However, you hold the buckle in case the horse should break free from the assistant.

Place your left foot in the stirrup and go through the motions

Mounting—reschooling to stand still.

of preparing to mount: Take hold of the front of the saddle or mane and the back of the saddle, and bounce once or twice on the ground with your right foot. Be sure that your toe in the stirrup does not dig into the horse's side. At this point, the horse will probably try to move off. Instead of mounting, say "Ho!" and remove your foot from the stirrup. Then have the assistant snatch sharply down on both reins. *Be certain that your foot is out of the stirrup before the assistant snatches the reins;* otherwise you could become caught in the stirrup and dragged if the horse tries to bolt.

When the horse is standing quietly, repeat. As long as he moves even a single step, do not attempt to mount, but repeat the command word as your assistant snatches, always being sure your foot is safely out of the stirrup first.

When the horse finally stands perfectly still, mount and settle quietly into the saddle. Do not move off, but stand still and after 30 seconds dismount and repeat. Have your assistant feed the horse pieces of carrot so he will associate being mounted and standing still with something pleasant.

Next have your assistant move away. Shorten your reins to the normal length for riding, being ready to snatch and say "Ho!" if the horse moves. As before, only mount when he stands perfectly still. Do not move off at a walk until he has stood perfectly still for 30 seconds.

Cause:

- ◆ The rider letting the horse move off at the walk—or worse, the trot—the instant he is in the saddle.
- ◆ The rider landing with a heavy thud in the saddle when he mounts, instead of settling lightly down.
- ◆ Pain—caused by badly fitting tack or a sore back that hurts. As the rider mounts, the horse tries to "run away" from the pain. If you suspect this, call a vet.

OVERBENDING

If your horse lowers his head from the base of his neck just above the withers and tucks in his chin, he is overbending or "over the bit." His face will be behind the vertical, with his nose closer to his chest than his forehead is.

Sometimes a horse who is overbending pulls, sometimes not. A horse overbending differs from a horse behind the bit: In the latter case the horse avoids contact with the bit at all if he can. A horse overbending is not necessarily afraid to meet the bit but has learned an odd position for his head and neck that he may be quite content to use, but that is not acceptable since it inhibits free forward movement.

Give quick, sharp little upward tugs on each rein, creating a vibrating motion, using first one rein, then the other, to discourage a horse from leaning downward on the bit. Give five or six tugs within the space of a second or two on one rein, while the other rein remains passive. His head will come up to a normal position. As he starts to drop his head again, repeat, using the other rein.

Be sure to maintain the speed and rhythm by using your legs. If you have been working in a medium trot, do not drop down to a slow trot, for instance. The horse will tend to slow down as you give the tugs on the rein. Riding at a trot up and down hills and over cavalletti poles on the ground will encourage him to extend his head and neck properly.

Do halt-to-trot transitions. In order for a horse to move from a standstill to a trot, he must use his hindquarters powerfully. As he does this, his hind end tends to become lower, and his forehand becomes elevated the equivalent amount, which helps to correct overbending.

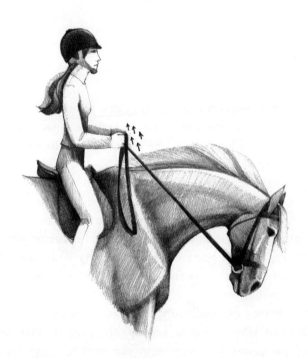

Overbending—raising the horse's head.

Cause:

♦ The rider is not maintaining impulsion forward (that is, not making the horse use his hind legs energetically).

♦ Resistance to some new signal (a horse being taught difficult new work may try this as the "answer" in an attempt to cause the rider to stop giving the signal).

♦ Heavy-handed riding (the rider pulling the horse's mouth constantly); the horse tries to find relief from the bit by placing his head in this position.

♦ A strong horse, determined to pull, may feel he will have less regulation from the rider and can pull more determinedly with his head in this position.

♦ The conformation of some horses—ewe-neck, for example—predisposes them to irregular head carriage.

PINNING EARS

If a horse pins his ears when he is ridden beside another horse it is often the first step toward biting or kicking. Snatch the rein and use a sharp word like "Hey!" (see Biting Other Horses While Being Ridden, page 31).

In the stable, before taking any action, be certain you know whether he is being merely bad-tempered or is genuinely frightened. A mistrustful horse who has been mistreated will only be more frightened by punishment and should never be punished.

Do not annoy a horse while he is eating. Even good-tempered horses prefer to eat in peace and may pin their ears if prevented from doing so.

If a horse, especially one who is normally good-tempered, pins his ears when being tacked up, the problem may be pain or fear of pain; suspect soreness in the mouth, a cut on the bars (gums), a spot rubbed sore under the bridle, tenderness in the

Correcting a horse who bites.

girth or saddle areas. If the soreness can be located, remove the cause. An unsheared sheepskin pad or girth cover can help alleviate discomfort in horses with tender backs or girth sores. If you suspect the pain is internal, call a vet.

If the problem is caused by fear, never punish the horse; be soothing and gentle with him to build his confidence. You can tell if the horse is frightened rather than merely bad-tempered, because a frightened horse will usually make an effort to get away from you when he pins his ears, and will not attempt to bite.

If the problem is bad temper and not fear, particularly if the horse actually attempts to bite, do the following: Give a sharp smack, hard, with the flat of your hand across the horse's nose, just above and to one side of the nostril, where the skin is soft and there is no bone close to the surface. Accompany this by a sharp word such as "Hey!" If the horse is on a leadshank, use a sharp snatch downward instead of a smack with your hand.

Never hit a horse on or near the head with anything except the flat of your hand. You will make him headshy and might injure an eye.

Cause:

- Bad temper, especially at feeding time
- Fear—if a horse has been mishandled, he may fear all people and pin his ears because he anticipates rough treatment
- The horse's annoyance at having a "socially inferior" horse approach or pass him while he is being ridden

PINNING A PERSON AGAINST THE WALL

If a horse begins to crowd you against the wall of a stall or other confined space, give a sharp smack with the flat of your hand on his neck, side, or hindquarters and say "Over!" If he is very stubborn, use a jumping bat instead of your hand, and give one or two quick, sharp taps. Never use the bat on or near his head, however, as you will make him headshy and could hit his eye. Do not use a bat on his legs, as it will encourage him to kick.

It is best to teach a horse to move away from you on command in the course of your regular work with him instead of attempting emergency measures in the closely confined quarters of a stall. A horse who does not understand the command "Over!" may become confused and move *toward* you simply because he does not understand what you mean.

Have him in a halter on a leadshank, in a paddock or ring where there is a clearly defined wall or fence. Stand him parallel to the fence but about 3 feet from it, and then, with your hand on his side, approximately where your calf would be if you were riding him, push him firmly toward the fence as you say "Over!" When he moves away from you, praise him. In the beginning, if he moves even a little bit, praise him so he will know that he is doing what you want, but gradually require him to move over quite boldly whenever you give the command and push with your hand on his side.

Teaching a horse to move away.

Never shout or become impatient with him. Always use the same tone of voice, and if your hand alone does not accomplish the result, use a bat or whip to reinforce the signal.

When the lesson is well learned on one side, repeat for the other. Then take him into the stall and repeat the exercise.

NOTE: Some people recommend keeping a stick in the stall that is long enough to protect you if you prop it between the crowding horse and the stall wall. It may be worth a try, but often either you won't have the stick handy or you won't have time to get it between the horse and wall before he has crowded you. Proper reschooling is less risky, and it is more likely to produce lasting results.

Cause:

- The horse lacks schooling.
- Fear—someone frightened the horse by shouting at him or punished him when he moved in the wrong direction due to confusion.

PROPPING

A prop is an abrupt, stiff-legged stop or sudden check in speed. Because the horse plants his front feet into the ground instead of shifting his weight back to use his hind legs to stop correctly, the prop is rough and jarring.

When the horse props, immediately push your heels down and forward, absorbing the jolt in your ankle joints, and bring your shoulders back to avoid being thrown forward.

Regain the pace you had before the prop occurred. Often after propping a horse may try to change the gait or the speed; for example, if he was trotting slowly, he may attempt to trot faster or to canter. Correct this without delay.

A prop may be the first step in refusal to go forward. If the horse shows any hesitation after propping, drive him on (see Balking—"Nappy," page 24). Propping, while not serious in itself as long as the rider has a secure seat, may lead to wheeling or rearing if uncorrected.

Cause:

- High spirits
- A startling sight, such as a shadow across the road
- A defensive reaction against too-rigid hands on the reins that "hang" on his mouth with constant, insensitive pressure

ALPHABETICAL LISTING OF PROBLEMS

PULLING

To correct a pulling horse, first decide what gait you want (walk, trot, or canter) and what speed you want (slow or medium).

Put pressure on both reins equally. Maintain a strong enough pressure to slow the horse to the speed you want. Keep the pressure smooth and steady; do not snatch the reins. You may have to pull quite hard at first, but do not ease up on the reins until the horse reaches the speed and the gait that you want. It may take many seconds at first before he responds and slows down. When the horse begins to go the speed you want, soften your hand—move your hands forward slightly, just an inch or so, or else merely open your fingers for a moment. This tells the horse that he has done what you want, since he no longer feels the unpleasant pull on his mouth which he felt while he was going too fast.

Be sure to remember to soften your hand. It is easy to forget to do this and simply to keep on pulling because you think the horse will speed up again as soon as you loosen the reins. But you must reward him by softening your hand the instant he slows to the correct speed, no matter how hard he is pulling.

As you repeat the exercise it will gradually take less time before he gives up resisting you. Finally—and this stage may not occur for several days or weeks—he will respond to a very light touch on the reins. Be alert for this, and use as little rein as you can.

Some people recommend using not a steady pull but rather a vibrating pull on the reins, which some horses find less easy to lean against. In some cases this may work better than a steady pull; try both and use whichever works best.

As long as the horse continues to go the speed you want, maintain light rein tension. But as soon as you feel him begin to increase his speed even a little, put pressure on his mouth until he returns to the correct speed. In this way, he will eventually realize that he can only avoid a hard, unpleasant pull, or an annoying vibrating pull, if he goes the speed you want. He will also learn that it does no good to pull against you, since he is never allowed to go faster when he does.

Taking a full-cross or a half-cross with your reins may help you hold them more firmly against a strong puller. For a full-cross, double the reins where you hold them instead of having each rein separate, and you will be better able to resist any side-to-side movements the horse may attempt, as well as the forward pull. If you make the cross short enough, you can brace your knuckles against the horse's neck and give some relief to your arms and shoulders. To soften your hand when holding the reins in this way, simply move the cross an inch or two up the crest of the neck toward the ears. If you take a half-cross, rather than a full-cross, you will be able to shorten the reins (see illustration below) while maintaining pressure on the reins.

It should be noted that a pulling horse, when he encounters firm pressure on the reins, will probably attempt to avoid the pressure by raising his head. As he raises his head, raise your

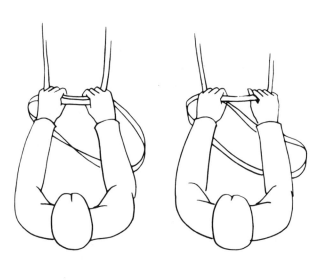

Left: Full-cross.   *Right:* Half-cross.

hands (see Above the Bit—"Stargazing," page 23) while you still maintain pressure on both reins. But be alert for the moment when he makes the smallest attempt to lower his head—perhaps a tiny "nod"—and reward that particular action by softening your hand for an instant before immediately continuing as before.

A good exercise to cure pulling is use of *transitions* (a change from one gait to another, or to a halt) because this teaches a horse to stop or slow down properly, on signal, using his hind legs. A young horse schooled in this way will never learn to pull. Even a habitual puller with a "hard" mouth can be taught not to pull. (Most so-called hard mouths are actually nothing more than the result of poor riding; a rider who constantly pulls on the horse's mouth even when he is going the proper speed soon teaches the horse that there is no escape from this punishment, and the horse will learn that there is no advantage in slowing down—in fact, he will probably try to go faster to see if he can escape the pulling in that way.)

Trot-to-halt transitions are particularly good because the trot

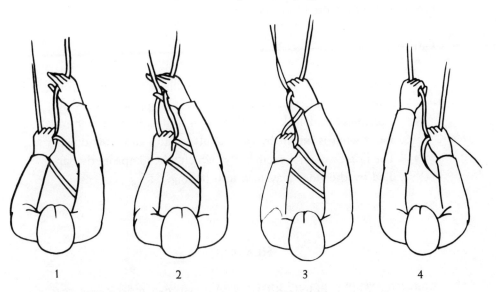

Shortening the reins. Half-Cross.

is an even, two-beat gait and it is easier to judge the speed and rhythm at this gait than at the walk or canter. Also, few horses pull at the walk, while at the canter many pull much harder than at the trot.

Begin trotting at a medium speed. When you have gone about ten steps, give the signal to halt. (Squeeze evenly with both reins and both legs, strongly enough to cause the horse to halt. As soon as he halts, cease the leg aids and soften your hand.)

When you have halted and let the horse stand for a second or two, go directly into a trot again (do not walk first). This causes him to use his hocks and hindquarters actively, which is important because he must learn to produce this energetic use of hind legs on command, and this is a clear way for him to understand what is expected of him. When he has made this association in his mind, it is possible to tell the horse to use his hind legs actively when he halts, as well as when he goes forward, by giving the same squeeze with your legs.

In this way your horse learns to halt properly. Any horse who can be properly halted does not pull.

Cause:

- ♦ "Heavy-handed" riding—the rider pulls without ever softening the hand even when the horse is doing what is asked
- ♦ Greenness and lack of schooling—confusion to the horse about what is meant by the signals to stop and slow down
- ♦ The horse's natural excitability, which when improperly handled by the rider may turn into pulling

REARING

REARING WHILE BEING RIDDEN. A horse can most easily rear when standing still or backing up. At the first sign of rearing, *drive the horse forward immediately and with great force.* Kick, spur, holler loudly, but make him move forward. Rearing is one of the most dangerous of vices, and if a horse learns it as a means of disobeying, he may at some time rear so high that he accidentally falls over backward on the rider.

Do not pull the reins at all. This would make the horse rear even higher, and might cause him to fall backward. Instead, throw your hands forward toward his neck and head, or hold the mane, to avoid any use of rein whatsoever.

As soon as his front feet come back to earth, drive him into a trot, then do a series of rapid halt-to-trot transitions, about six steps each, to occupy his mind and body fully so he cannot think

Rearing—throwing the hands forward.

about rearing again. Be severe with a horse who rears, and make his association with rearing unpleasant.

Some people recommend turning the horse rapidly in one or two quick circles before forcing him energetically forward after a rear. If you do this, do not always turn him in the same direction or he may learn to wheel quickly after he rears, having learned to do so by frequent repetitions in one direction.

Check his mouth for injury. If teeth need floating or his mouth is sore, or if a curb chain has rubbed a raw spot, remove the cause.

NOTE: The following actions in dealing with a rearing horse are *not* recommended:

- Hitting the horse on the head as he rears, with a stick, hose, or other hard object. This may cause permanent injury.
- Turning the horse in tight circles until he becomes dizzy. Some horses lose their balance and fall over.
- Deliberately pulling the reins as the horse rears in order to make him fall over backward and frighten himself; this is extremely dangerous and foolhardy. The rider may intend to get off at the last moment, and failing to do so, be badly hurt.

REARING WHILE BEING LED. If a horse rears while being led, he will usually attempt to run backward as soon as his front feet hit the ground.

To prevent his getting free, *move with him as he backs up.* Do not attempt to hold a horse in place by pulling on a leadshank or the reins as you lead him; he can easily outpull you and pull free.

The following procedures must *always* be used. When leading a horse by the bridle, take the reins over his head and lead him as described in Leading—Balking, page 74. If leading with a halter, always use a leadshank, as described in Leading—Balking, page 74.

If a horse rears while being led, attach a leadshank with

Proper adjustment of leadshank on a horse who rears.

1-foot chain so that it passes over the nose of the horse (see illustration, page 97). When he rears, go with him until he stops rearing and running back, then immediately give three or four very sharp snatches straight downward on the leadshank or reins. This will make the horse raise his head abruptly to avoid the downward pressure. He may even rear again. If so, simply repeat, a little more severely than the first time. In cases where the horse has learned this habit very well—a "professional" rearer—have an assistant stand nearby with a longe whip and repeat the process, while the assistant gives the horse several sharp flicks of the whip above his hocks. Be prepared for the horse to lash out with his hind feet. A horse who requires correction of this severity will not willingly relinquish this form of defense. However if you persevere and make the punishment severe enough, the horse will eventually realize that it is not worth the effort to resist you in this way.

Be certain, however, that you are ready for his initial reactions; he will most certainly try to kick, and he may also try to bite. The severity of the downward snatch with reins or leadshank and the swiftness with which you punish are the keys to correction of rearing while being led.

Cause:

- Horse not being corrected for refusal to go forward, leading to rearing as a means of avoiding work he does not like
- Fear—a horse may rear if suddenly confronted with something he considers dangerous that he did not see until he was very close to it
- Exuberance and high spirits, especially in young horses
- Pain due to mouth injury, curb chain, or teeth in need of floating

REINBACK—HINDQUARTERS SWING

See also Reinback—Refusal to Move at All, page 99.

As the horse steps backward, if the hindquarters swing to the right, bring the right rein to the right—that is, use direct right rein, moving your right hand away from the horse's shoulder. Put the same amount of light pressure on the right rein as on the left rein as you move it. Use both legs with equal pressure to ask for the step backward (see illustration, page 99).

Keep your reins 10 inches or more apart as you ask for the reinback. If you do this there is less chance of the horse swinging his quarters, and you can correct the problem more quickly if he does.

Do not attempt to straighten the horse's quarters with your leg. He will almost certainly overcorrect, as the hindquarters move easily in a sideways direction and it is difficult to obtain a slight enough reaction to the leg.

Cause:

- Lack of schooling, greenness
- Rider attempting to pull the horse backward with the rein instead of driving him onto an unmoving hand until he steps backward

REINBACK.

Correction for swinging of quarters.

REINBACK—REFUSAL TO MOVE AT ALL

If the reinback is properly performed, the horse steps backward smoothly and quietly without resisting each time the rider puts a light pressure on both reins equally and squeezes with both legs. The horse's legs move exactly as they do in the trot, only in reverse: diagonal pairs (the right fore and left hind at the same time, then the other diagonal pair, or vice versa).

If the horse refuses to move at all, opens his mouth, or raises his head when you give the signal to reinback, *increase your leg, not your hand.* A sharp tap with a whip just behind your calf will help in most cases (use a dressage whip or gaited-horse whip, which is long enough so that you need not remove your hand from the rein to use it).

Never try to pull the horse backward. Instead drive him forward onto an unmoving hand, and when he steps back a complete step (that is, each diagonal pair moves once) reward him by ceasing the signal momentarily.

Each step should be asked for separately. Do not allow the horse to run backwards in a series of steps. If requested smoothly, there will be no hesitation or unevenness in his steps.

If you are unable to get the horse to take a step backward even when you use your legs and the whip, he probably does not understand the meaning of the signal. In this case, give the signal again, clearly but gently, and as you squeeze with your legs, have an assistant tap gently with a whip on the horse's chest just above the foreleg, or at the top of the foreleg itself. When the horse moves back one complete step, walk immediately forward, being sure you reward him promptly by softening your hands for a moment as you go forward. Then halt and repeat. When he will do one step easily, add another, then begin to vary the number of steps you ask for, so that he must respond precisely to your signals and therefore does not learn to run backward hastily.

If you do not have an assistant, stand beside the horse and tap his chest or foreleg with a whip as you squeeze both reins with the other hand. When he understands the rein signal, mount and repeat, using your legs properly as you use the reins. Gradually use only enough rein to block forward movement, and enough leg to make him rein back correctly.

Cause:

- ◆ Greenness
- ◆ Improper schooling
- ◆ The rider pulling the horse backward rather than driving him forward onto an unmoving hand

REINBACK—RUNNING BACKWARD IN A SERIES OF STEPS

Give the signal for one step of reinback by squeezing with both legs, keeping your hands still while maintaining a very slight pressure on the reins. When the horse has stepped backward one complete step (each diagonal pair of legs moves once) move your hands forward so that there can be no accidental rein pressure, and drive the horse energetically forward into a trot.

Many horses shown regularly in hunter classes learn to count three steps backward followed by three forward, because they frequently follow this pattern in a show ring. A smart judge may ask for a specific number of steps such as two or four, and such horses will not know how to perform this task as they have not been taught the reinback signal correctly—that is, to respond with a single complete step for each signal.

If you ride across country, difficult terrain may make it essential that you be able to ask for, and get, a single step in the reinback. Suppose your horse has jumped a ditch but stopped in front of a fence running parallel to it a few feet farther on. In order to jump the fence you must back your horse precisely two steps; if he backs three steps, you will back into the ditch. In such a case you must be able to ask for, and get, precisely the number of steps you require.

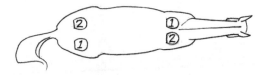

REINBACK.

Top: Footfall sequence.

Bottom: Reining back correctly.

HORSE SENSE

Cause:

♦ Incorrect schooling by the rider

ROLLING WHILE BEING RIDDEN

If your horse stops and begins pawing with his front hoof while being ridden through water or sand, he is probably about to roll. Unless you take quick action, his front legs will begin to buckle and he will lie down and roll.

Drive him forward energetically with your leg or whip. A horse can roll only if he is allowed to stand still. As you drive him forward, pull his head upward with the reins.

Rolling while being ridden. Use of whip and rein.

Cause:

◆ The horse wanting to scratch his back or cool off in water on a hot day

RUNNING BACKWARD WHILE BEING RIDDEN

There are two methods of curing this problem.

The first is to drive the horse vigorously forward with leg and whip, following the same methods as those recommended for Balking—"Nappy," page 24.

A second, and often very effective, correction may be used. Only use this correction, however, if the horse is running backward because he has learned this vice in order to avoid work, and not because he is facing something of which he is genuinely afraid. For example, if your horse sees an umbrella several yards ahead and begins to hesitate, he is probably afraid—drive him forward with leg and whip. But if you ride a horse into a ring and without any apparent reason he begins to run backward, he has probably learned a bad habit, which he uses to avoid work. In that case, do the following:

Let the horse run backward as long as he wishes. When he finally stops, do not allow him to stand still, but insist that he *continue* to back up, and keep on backing him until he wants very much to stop. Finally, when he is very tired of backing up, drive him forward into a trot with your legs and whip.

If the horse shows any tendency to rear, however, do *not* use this correction, and follow the correction for Rearing, page 94.

Cause:

◆ Fear
◆ Desire to avoid work

HORSE SENSE

♦ Failure by the rider to correct refusal to go forward when it first occurs; if uncorrected this habit may easily develop into running backward

RUNNING BACK WHILE TIED

It is a good plan never to tie your horse to anything unless he is in an enclosed space, such as a stall or trailer, and cannot run backward and break the leadshank or his halter. *Never* tie a horse by the reins; in addition to breaking a bridle, he can damage his mouth. When saddling, slip the reins over your arm as you work. Prevention is the key, as a horse can break almost anything you tie him with and many soon learn to do so.

If you do decide to cure a horse who has learned to run back, be sure that you proceed with caution. First, have a very strong, soft rope; if you use a sisal rope or a nylon longeline, you run danger of causing sore rope marks or, more seriously, of having the rope or line slip, making the horse panic. Use the very strong, smooth rope available in hardware or boat-supply stores, which cannot chafe and will withstand 4,000 pounds of pressure.

Tie the rope around his girth, just behind his elbows, like a surcingle, snugly but not tightly. *Make sure that the knot will not slip and tighten accidentally when the horse pulls backward.* Use a square knot, and knot it several times to be sure. The knot will be under his girth, just behind his front legs. Now take the rest of the rope and run the end through the halter under the chin (not through the throatlatch of the halter, as this may break).

Attach the rope to an immovable object, such as a telephone pole or a large tree trunk lying on the ground, but do not use a fence post or a machine, because a struggling horse can move even a car or a trailer. Be sure to choose something that doesn't have even a remote chance of being moved. Using a quick-release knot (see illustration, page 105), attach the horse with no more than 4 feet of rope between the halter and the object. It is more awkward for him to pull strongly against something on the ground than something at shoulder level where he could use all his weight to pull straight back.

Running back when tied.

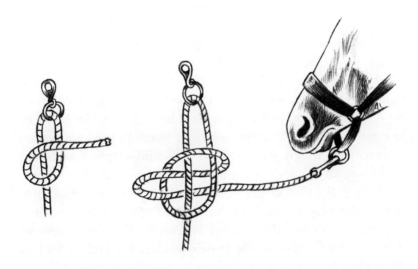

Quick-release knot.

Let the horse struggle until he stops fighting and will stand quietly. Then praise him while he is still tied up. Repeat for several days. Eventually he will associate a rope hanging to the ground with having to remain still, and you will be able to "ground tie" him (that is, leave the reins over his head hanging to the ground).

NOTE: *Never under any circumstances tie a rope around the horse's neck.* The knot may slip and choke him. If the horse is choking and panics it may be impossible to come to his aid and he could die before you could get the rope off.

Cause:

♦ Fear of being restrained
♦ Habit learned from experimentation and finding that he can break anything to which he is tied

SHYING

If a horse sees something on his right that frightens him, he will usually shy to the left, and vice versa.

If he shies to the left, pull the right rein sideways to the right (direct right rein), moving it well away from the horse's neck; be sure not to pull straight back, but sideways. An easy way to remember is simply to *move your hand toward the object that frightens the horse.* Take a fairly short hold on both reins—perhaps one-third of the way up the neck. Keep light pressure on both reins.

As you use the direct right rein, press the left rein snugly against the neck on an angle that would cross the withers if it were long enough (the indirect left rein). This helps prevent "rubbernecking"—that is, the horse's bending his neck to look at the frightening object while moving his body away from it.

While using direct and indirect reins, use the leg on the side away from the object (in this case, your left leg) and push the horse toward what frightens him. Use your voice confidently as you approach something you think may scare your horse. Your attitude of confidence will help reassure him (see illustration below).

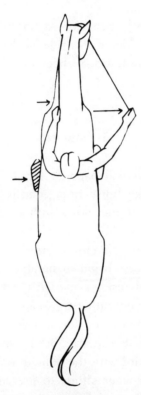

SHYING.

Correction of attempt to shy to the left.

Cause:

- ♦ Fear of a strange object—sudden movements, even smells blown suddenly toward a horse
- ♦ Shadows on a road

- The rider tensing up when he sees something he thinks will frighten the horse; this alone may cause a horse to shy when he otherwise would not
- High spirits and playfulness
- In rare cases, poor eyesight. If you suspect this, call the vet
- Roguish "naughty" behavior—a horse who has learned he can unseat and "dump" his rider when he decides to, may become quite professional about shying

STUMBLING

This is not a vice, but if it happens use the emergency measure given here to keep the horse from actually falling with you, if possible, as a horse that goes down with a rider can cause serious injury. However, if your horse stumbles frequently, have a good vet examine him for possible unsoundness.

If you feel your horse begin to stumble on his front legs, get his head up immediately using a smooth steady pull on the reins—that is, do not snatch, but rather try to *lift* the horse's head.

Push your heels down and forward as you do this and lean back somewhat so that you can brace strongly against being pulled down and forward with the reins. But if you find the horse is going down despite your efforts to prevent it, kick both feet free of the stirrups and jump off.

If a horse stumbles on his hind legs, allow full use of his head and neck to act as a counterbalance. If he is going down, jump off.

In general, ride a horse who tends to stumble with more collection than usual—keep his hocks under him and avoid letting him shuffle along on the forehand. Exercises that encourage active use of the hocks, such as trot-to-halt and halt-to-trot transitions, may help. Also, riding up and down hills at a trot may encourage a lazy or careless horse to pay more attention. If you ride in winter or must ride on hard roads, have your horse shod with *borium*, a very hard metal placed in dots on the bottom of the shoe, giving traction. Ask your blacksmith about special corrective shoeing.

Cause:

- Bad footing—mud, ice, loose sand on a hard surface, or slick hard-top roads.
- Feet too long—have the horse reshod.
- Holes—avoid going fast in country that may have holes that are not visible until you are upon them.
- Unsoundness—bad shoulders, legs, or back could cause a horse to stumble frequently. If the situation is chronic and the horse stumbles even where the ground is level, suspect unsoundness.
- Illness—the horse is sick or has internal pains, worms, or damage to internal organs. Have a vet check him.
- Clumsiness—like people some horses are simply clumsy and would just as happily go down as make any major effort to stay on their feet. Sometimes young horses, especially if broken to ride too young, exhibit a tendency to clumsiness and later outgrow it.
- Unfitness—horse being asked to do work too strenuous for his muscle condition.

NOTE: Some people say that it is better to give a horse his head when he stumbles on his front legs, and that he uses his head and neck in regaining his balance. However, experience seems to show that horses who are given their heads when they stumble on the forehand just as often go down all the way, while those whose heads are pulled up often regain their balance.

HORSE SENSE

TRAILERS—REFUSAL TO LOAD

By far the best cure is prevention: If you have a trailer, keep it in the pasture and feed the horse inside it until he has no fear and will walk into and back out of it willingly. Let the horse back out as soon as he wants to. Finally, when he is perfectly used to the whole process of getting on and off, do up the chain behind him and let him stand there a few minutes while you praise him. Be sure the front end of the trailer is securely propped up so the trailer cannot tip forward when the horse walks into it.

Never fasten the horse's head until you have secured him with a chain behind him or closed the ramp. A horse who runs back, pulling to free his head, will hit the ceiling of the trailer violently and perhaps even fatally.

Sometimes it helps to accustom a horse to walking on a piece of plywood on the ground first, which may make him less afraid of stepping onto the ramp of a trailer for the first time.

However, if you must load a horse who has learned to fear or dislike trailers, do the following: Turn the trailer so the sun shines into it, rather than into the horse's eyes. If he can see into the interior, it will make him less afraid of going into it. Be sure the ramp is on solid ground, that it is not slippery, and that the front is securely propped up so it can not tip forward. Have a person inside the trailer, with oats or other bribes, holding a long lead-rope attached to the horse. As the horse moves forward, the person inside the trailer should keep the rope snug by taking up the slack, but should not try to pull him forward, as this merely makes a horse more resistant. He should only keep the horse straight and try to lure him into the trailer. At the same time, two more people stretch another rope behind the horse, pressing against his hindquarters just above the hocks. They should stand about six feet apart as they press the horse forward with the rope, and should be careful to avoid getting kicked if the horse lashes out with his feet. Another person can sometimes add momentum by applying some swats with a broom to the horse's hind end.

ALPHABETICAL LISTING OF PROBLEMS

You cannot force a horse into a trailer; rather you must limit his options, making all except the one you want unpleasant for him (see illustration below).

However, again it should be noted that the best method by far is proper education in the first place, and it is easy to see that the above method, while it will eventually succeed in loading a balking horse, will not serve to make him feel very happy about the whole subject of trailers.

NOTE: Some people advise the use of tranquilizers. This can be risky, however; if the horse becomes too "dopey" his reactions slow down and he may fall or injure himself when traveling.

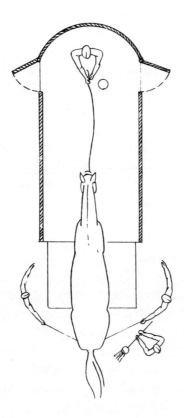

Loading into a trailer.

Cause:

- Horse might lack proper education.
- Fear—the horse may have had a bad experience traveling, or have slipped off the ramp while unloading. If the day is very bright, the interior of the trailer may look dark and mysterious to a horse.

TURNS AND CIRCLES—CUTTING IN, WRONG BEND, REFUSAL TO MOVE OUT

Trot the horse in a turn or circle to the left. Take a short enough left rein so that the horse must bend his head and neck slightly to the left and cannot turn it to the right. Use indirect rein—that is, on a line from his mouth to your left hand which, if the rein were long enough, would eventually cross the withers (see illustration 2, page 114). His head, neck, and backbone from head to tail must be curved toward the left the same degree as the turn or circle that he is making. Hold the left rein firmly; if necessary, hook your thumb over the horse's withers and be sure he cannot pull the rein from your grip. He will probably resist this inside rein very strongly at first.

Squeeze with your left leg, or if necessary dig into his left side with your heel. The horse should move away from the pressure of your leg. (If he does not do this readily, teach him to do so as explained in Pinning a Person Against the Wall, page 88).

Take your right rein to the right, leading the horse outward from the center of the circle (direct right rein). Be careful not to allow him to bend to the right, however; the left rein should prevent this (see illustration 2, page 114).

Keep your right leg slightly behind the girth. If the horse

swings his hindquarters to the right, push them back on the curve of the circle.

NOTE: Since you must sometimes take a strong hold on the reins—especially at first when the horse is very resistant—be sure to soften your hand as often as you can by moving your hands slightly forward or simply opening your fingers momentarily to remove the pressure on the bit and reward him for responding correctly. *Soften your hand whenever the horse is bending correctly or moving out on the circle, or both.*

It helps to alternate the pressure on each rein—that is, first lead the horse out on the circle with the right direct rein (while the left rein remains passive); next make the left indirect rein active to remind the horse to keep the correct bend (while the right rein remains passive).

It is important to remember to soften your hand, because if you simply put strong pressure on the reins and do not release the pressure when the horse is attempting to do what you ask, you cause two undesired results. First, you teach the horse that no matter what he does you will continue to pull on his mouth, so there is no advantage to his moving out on the circle or having the correct bend. The horse will eventually develop a "dead" mouth—he will be simply trying to ignore a signal that seems to have no answer.

Second, you destroy free forward movement, the horse's steps become cramped and uneven, and you bring out his worst movement instead of his best.

However, do not soften your hand (except as described in alternating the active use of each hand) until the horse responds correctly. If, for instance, he is still cutting into the circle instead of moving out as you are asking him to do, and he still has not bent properly to the left for the left-handed circle, then do not soften your hands. Only soften the pressure on his mouth when he conforms, even momentarily, to what you ask him to do, either by moving out on the circle, or bending correctly, or both.

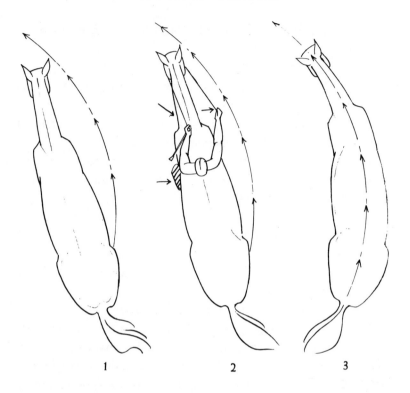

1   2   3

CORRECTING THE BEND AND MOVING THE HORSE OUT ON A TURN OR CIRCLE.

Left: Incorrect bend.   *Center:* Using left leg, indirect left rein, direct right rein.   *Right:* Horse bent correctly, moved out on circle.

Cause:

- ◆ Green horses being asked to make turns that are too small for their degree of suppleness
- ◆ Lack of correction by the rider due to lack of knowledge

ALPHABETICAL LISTING OF PROBLEMS

WHEELING

This is similar to shying, except that the horse shifts his weight to his hind legs and uses them as a pivot to turn. Use the same correction as for Shying, page 106, but also keep your reins separated by about 10 inches. As the horse tries to wheel to the right, bring your left rein away from the neck and force him to turn his head to the left. At the same time, keep your right rein snug enough so the horse cannot "rubberneck" (that is, simply bend his neck flexibly around). By keeping the right rein snug, and by pulling the left rein to the left, you can move his front half to the left, the opposite direction from which he was attempting to wheel.

As you use your reins, use your heel on his right side to force him to move his hindquarters also to the left.

When you have corrected a wheeling horse, drive him forward again in the direction you were going before the problem occurred, but be ready for him to attempt to wheel again.

Cause:

- ◆ Fear of an unexpected object close at hand
- ◆ A bad habit learned due to lack of correction

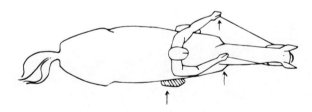

WHEELING.

Correction of attempt to wheel to the right: left direct rein, right indirect rein, right leg.

INDEX

INDEX